Permissions: info@loveacrystal.com
https://www.loveacrystal.com

Publisher: Lila Gems
ISBN: 979-8-9866921-0-4
Printed in the United States of America

A CIP catalogue record for this book is available from the Library of Congress under
CRYSTAL-CLEAR JOY!
© 2022 Sandra Muller

Cover Photograph © 2022 Sandra Müller
Cover design Art Director: Mark Sagato
Interior Book Design: Emy Farella
Cover photographer: Sandra Müller
Back cover portrait: Lorraine Young photography
Courtesy of Sandra Müller

MEDICAL DISCLAIMER: The following information is intended for general information purposes only. Individuals should always see their health care provider before administering any suggestions made in this book. Any of this application of the material set forth in the following pages is at the reader's discretion and his or her sole responsibility.

A SHAMANIC JOURNEY HOME TO

CRYSTAL-CLEAR

JOY!

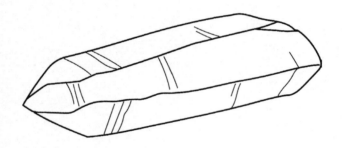

CHANNELED CONVERSATIONS WITH

THE COUNCIL OF AR

SANDRA MÜLLER

"Be the solution!
Be the one who emanates the
Freedom you want,
the Love you want,
the Abundance of Spirit
that you want to see
for this entire Planet Earth!
Be the solution!"

THE COUNCIL of AR

CONTENTS

Channeled INTRODUCTION to The COUNCIL of AR

"We, THE COUNCIL of AR, would like to introduce ourselves so that your experience of reading this book can be pleasant, and the understanding of our messages can find a clear and unobstructed path past the constant chatter of your mind.

We are energy beings or Spirits, that after many centuries have been assigned to the evolution of human beings on Planet Earth.
We are your constant guardians and caregivers.

Our energies adopt various shapes and forms so that each individual, who comes in contact with us as a Spirit form, will be at ease with that particular shape or form, given their cultural beliefs and faiths. But with that being said, we are all one, no matter what shape, or form you visualize us in.

We are energy, pure energy, pure love, and the constant caregivers for all human beings and all existing beings, including animals, insects, plants, trees, and all who exist in some shape or form.

Our powers are applicable to all since we are the ones who orchestrate this symphony called life.

As part of this auspicious introduction, we would also like to acknowledge that life in other galaxies is in full action at this point, and has been for all eternity, and endless time.

We would like to introduce your hearts to all beings that exist. The ones you are able to acknowledge at this time, and the ones you have never thought possible to exist.
There are millions of beings alive in and all around your galaxy, and in millions of other stars, planets, and galaxies.

For centuries, humans have been curious regarding the subject of possible life on other Planets, and we feel that now is the opportune time, and opening of such information.

This book is not about this subject necessarily, there will be more books channeled by Sandra in the future that will give you more advanced information regarding this subject.

We feel that it is appropriate at this time, as you begin to glance at these pages, that you allow your hearts to open to new information that might shock you in some ways, but that may also invigorate your being, and allow you to receive your own memories and telepathic downloads that your subconscious being has stored for you until the time is right.

Today is the right time for you to receive more expansion and openness in the smaller thoughts you have allowed so far.

Please read this book with an open heart. You do not need to use your energy to agree or disagree with our deliverances.

The information given in this book is not out of reach for you even if you are a beginner in your ascension process.
You are fully capable at this point of absorbing any given information that we have allowed in this book.

This is just the beginning; these chapters will help you open to new horizons that have been obstructed by your fear of the unknown.

It is time to lift your protective veils.
By doing this you will be relieved of so much pain.
The pain you have been carrying for centuries due to your mistrust and self-created thoughts that good and bad exist.

This concept is entirely false: your enemy is no one but yourself. You are fighting only with yourselves. You are your own and only enemy.
All of creation is playing roles in the theater of life so that you, as a Soul, can have an experience.
During a lifespan, you will take on various roles that will activate various parts of you and help you fulfill the contract you

had assigned for yourself before your current incarnation.

You are just a puppet playing out your contract so that you can be embellished with the layers of the constant evolution of your own Soul, and so that this may happen in accordance with the game of life, your own Lila.

We ask you to enter into this new realm with little, or no judgment of any kind.

Your intellect is full of ideas regarding what you think is right or wrong. But we assure you that these chapters will help you understand your life, and all lives happening at this moment in time, with a broader vision.

In any event, this is our intention for bringing this book to life.

Those who are suffering are under our constant care. We are the true caregivers, we are the true lovers, we are the true healers. We are always available to appease the hearts of all who exist.
Take a moment to allow our most compassionate and pure love to enter your hearts.

We hope that you will enjoy these chapters. Our words are imbued with our benevolent loving frequency.

Sandra has been our scribe, she has received and recorded our words. These are not her ideas or words.
This is our way of communicating with you.
Blessings to all. "

"IN YOUR NEXT BREATH, WE EXIST."

THE COUNCIL of AR

*"We discover in you
the same limitations that
we know so well.
Again and again, until the heart
allows us to come close and hold you.
Grant us your acceptance,
so that we can immerse you in
our love, and blessings.
No need to lead the way,
we have the lanterns.
We are the ones that can
light the path for you."*

THE COUNCIL of AR

CHAPTER ONE

LET'S TALK ABOUT THIS BOOK

HOW DID THIS BOOK COME ABOUT?

During a Shamanic Journey, I see myself with both of my power animals, the ones I know and love so much. I see myself combing the fur of my Power Animal. I remove several ticks that are sucking his blood.

"Is this an analogy for how I am feeling?" I ask him.

"Yes, many external nuisances are draining you at this time. Don't let them in."

"Please help me, please take me to the Upper World", I ask. My Power Animal takes me on the customary ride to get to the Upper World. I enter the Upper World and see all my Helping Spirits waiting for us. I bow down and greet each one with love, and respect.

I am humbled by the shame of how low I feel. Sadness is overpowering. " Please help me", I ask.

I am given healing by one of the Helping Spirits. She performs surgery on my chest cavity. My heart is black as charcoal. She replaces it with a new heart, red like fire, pumping with life. My Helping Spirit sucks my veins, and spits out my blood. I am then given new blood from a transparent jar.

The new blood is so alive, it wiggles by itself.

The entire COUNCIL of AR is thrilled, and starts clapping with JOY! I am sewn back together. They now push a start button.

Funny! I have been jump-started again! I sit down and look at THE COUNCIL of AR in awe. They show me a book. "I am going to write a book?" I ask.

"Yes!" They say.

"Ok", I answer.

"How do I start?" I ask.

"Just start with this channeling."

"Once upon a time, many centuries ago, your Soul came into existence for the first time. Born from tiny energy that pushed itself to have a space in the big Universe. You, as all, were conceived this way. Millions of years ago. Conceived for the sole purpose of life exploration, and to experience JOY!

As the contracts are put in place for a particular incarnation,

Souls must choose their levels of difficulty. No pressure, but a constant incentive is given to include the harder lessons. This will help the Soul accumulate more useful experiences, linked to other Souls that you call Soulmates or Soul collaborators.

There will always be pain involved in a lifespan. There will always be obstacles and illusions to overcome.

Each day the energies will fluctuate, driven also by the location of the star systems that have special affinities to each Soul.

Thin protective membranes encapsulate the body, but the location of a particular star will pierce these membranes with their various energies.

Daily, the Soul, encased inside a vessel, will be activated by sensations, thoughts, dreams, and memories. These will deliver JOY or fear and confusion, or simple moments of nothingness.

This constant fluctuation is a necessary part of life in Earthschool. No one escapes! No one.

The ego and the intellect also play a big part as well.

Distant memories of moments filled with love also come to haunt you, adding certain elements, feelings, emotions, and nostalgic remembrance.

Every day at Earthschool will be different from the other. Feelings of helplessness and sorrow are created by external facts that life offers as well. No one will be free of pain.

Pain exists as a catalyst to help each Soul make sense of it all. So when you feel caught in an uncomfortable moment or situation, have the strength to ask the Universe these questions:

- *What am I learning from myself at this moment?*
- *What memories or feelings have triggered sadness in me?*
- *What, or where is my path to return to the JOY inside of me?*
- *What will I accomplish with the experiences and process that I am navigating through?*
- *Where is wisdom inside of me, and how can I gain it back when I lose my stable ground?*
- *How can I shine my light again, and how can I help others retrieve theirs?*
- *How can I be filled with my own love, so that I do not feel the need to feed on the energies of others, like a vampire?*
- *How can I learn to love myself, and fulfill my existence, so that I can be with others in total freedom?*
- *Freedom of love, freedom from ego, freedom from fear, freedom from envy, freedom from manipulative strategies.*
- *How can I embody my own fountain of love, JOY, and creativity?*

*"JOY is available even to
the saddest hearts!
Given that laughter and dream-state
are always available.
Just close your eyes, and envision
something JOY-full, and the JOY will
penetrate your field.
JOY is accessible to all,
it just takes a little effort to
jumpstart the process.
Just a little smile, a little daydreaming
will take you inside where
CRYSTAL-CLEAR JOY resides!"*

THE COUNCIL of AR

"Could you give me a title for the book?"

During a Shamanic Journey, I am shown a peace sign on the third eye. My Power Animal allows me to caress him. I caress his beautiful fur, it's cold outside, it's snowing. He takes me up to a glacier and we climb it.

We reach a flat area where a Sun is coming out. It is the Central Sun! I recognize him with excitement in my heart!
There is a big icy slide, and we jump on it, and slide inside the Central Sun!

"I am home! I am Home!" I exclaim with JOY!

*"A Shamanic Journey Home, to CRYSTAL-CLEAR JOY!
Channeled conversations with THE COUNCIL of AR, is the title of the book!"* The Central Sun answers.
The Spirit of the Central Sun wants to talk.

"Hello, I am the Central Sun. I am you, you are me. We are creating together. I do not exist without something to create. You are my creation. I have made you out of love, to connect you back home, to experience CRYSTAL-CLEAR JOY at the same time as you are existing on Planet Earth for a limited time. You are all able to access both dimensions simultaneously.

A lifeless body is just a container, empty of Soul, of essence and Spirit. These have departed and gone back home.

We, THE COUNCIL of AR, and the Central Sun are one. Just like you are one with us. You, meaning your Soul, and your Spirit.

The body or vessel is just a beautiful creation we have put together. A sensory container with many self-sustained living molecules that can function individually to maintain life in this living creation, your body, or vessel.

This is a gift, so that your essence can be encased in an apparatus able to experience, and exist for a limited time, since density on Planet Earth is very heavy, compared to what your essence is used to, and this can be very tiring for the Soul.

Some Souls can only sustain this density for a limited time. They choose shorter live spans that will be just enough to have access to the experiences and the lessons they had volunteered to endure."

*"In the breath,
exists all the Magic."*

THE COUNCIL of AR

CHAPTER TWO

FROM FEELING PAIN TO ACCESSING JOY!

"Why is our Soul's evolution so important?"

"The experience of constant evolution is what the Soul ultimately yearns for, trains for, and anticipates with great fervor. It is the potential put into action. It is the goal.

Imagine being an actor that never finds an audience. The actor has a natural passion or eagerness to perform, and the audience gives him or her the fuel needed to engage and express this natural fervor in a song, or a play.

The Soul has various creative passions, and can only explore them whilst in a body, or a vessel. The talents are innate.

When a Soul needs a break, it can also choose a vessel that is less enthusiastic, or talented. In that case, the Soul will be more inclined to observe. To learn through observation."

*"There is no life given
to a Soul in vain.
There is always a purpose."*

THE COUNCIL of AR

"What is the true nature of a human being?"

"The true nature of a human being is to explore the various experiences that are available in human form. This entails: Encountering fear, solving problems within the dynamic of creativity, restoring a link to Universal laws, and working within those Universal laws.

Accepting the challenges as opportunities that allow higher learnings according to the capabilities of that Soul, and within the limitations of the contracts made before birth, such as; personality, temperament, character, intelligence, ego, emotional maturity, natural talents and abilities given to each Soul, as a gift from the Divine Source, for the sole purpose of Soul evolution.

Since not every Soul takes on the same challenges at the same time, there is always every nuance continuously in motion.

This allows vessels in human form to have all dramas occurring in the same period, and creates an interesting mix of experiences activated during the same era!"

"Why is there always so much suffering?"

"Because there is no evolution under continuous utopian ideologies and experiences.

The vessel or human body is always allowed to experience blissful and very powerful moments of connection, of full integration to high frequencies that, in themselves, configure the fuel needed to understand, and accept the challenges.

There also need to be Souls that accept horrific lives, due not only to karmic debts, but to help others discern where good and bad reside."

*"May your vessel merge with
the Divine presence
that inhabits each one
of your molecules.
May this merging show you
the Magic!"*

THE COUNCIL of AR

"What about depression?"

"Depression is just loss of power. Loss of connection to Universal guidance, when the ego kicks in and wants to lead, and the doors start closing, one after the other.

This beautiful Universe is just showing you that something is off by allowing feelings of utter displeasure to enter your field.

At that point, one must surrender and know that you are pushing the un-pushable.

To access flow, one must connect back to Source and the heart."

*"Tame the ego so that it
does not control you.
Allow your Spirit to lead the way.
Remain an observer with
no entanglements.
Connect to your inner state of JOY
through the wisdom of your already
learned experiences.
Become an observer of your existence
so that you can align
yourself back
when your footing stumbles on
the wrong pebble."*

THE COUNCIL of AR

"How can one access flow?"

"Soul retrieval, nature contemplation, music, dance, sleep, meditation, conscious breath, Earth grounding, silence, and most of all, trust, acceptance, and surrender.

Reset the direction of your mainsail for the wind to kick in again, and guide you with no doubts, no confusion, and/or distortions. One must allow.

We can then grant you more love which will enter your field while you sleep, and your cells can receive it without judgment. Furthermore, we can envelop your body with the pungent smell of a perfect rose so that you can become filled, and your cells can rejuvenate.

We can also add in you a little fervor for life when your stamina is low. We know how it is to be human, most of us have had this experience.

Rejoice in knowing that We, THE COUNCIL of AR are with you at all times. Even while you sleep, when you travel so far and deep into other realms."

*"We dance with the Divine
within you,
within your breath,
and the life field that you are.
We rescue the ones who are drowning
in their stubbornness,
thinking they can control life!"*

THE COUNCIL of AR

"What is the difference between the Soul, and the Spirit?"

"The Soul is the entanglement that links a vessel to its higher self. The Soul has traits of personalities, moods, memories, defects, and talents.

The Soul is like the fuel, or battery, that keeps the vessel alive. A vessel is lifeless once the Soul leaves to journey back home. The Soul keeps records of each experience the vessel is exposed to.

The Soul is connected to its own Spirit, and that Spirit is directly connected to Source or God. So, the Spirit is the connecting link to Source.

Meanwhile, the Soul can divide into various Souls, or fragments, to facilitate alternative experiences for a vessel.

The Soul leaves the body while the vessel sleeps, but a secondary Soul stays, to keep all the bodily functions mechanically working and to keep the vessel alive.

Soul loss can happen due to trauma, extreme sadness, fear, or other conditions the vessel might experience during an incarnation.
So it is important to understand that the Soul can lose its vitality and strength during the lifespan of an individual.

In shamanic healing, Soul parts can be brought back to complete the Soul, to return it to its original vibrant state of life force.

This ultimately is of great significance. It is important to understand that Soul loss can encompass, or bring about disease, addiction, depression, and ultimately conscious or unconscious deliberate need to end a life before its natural date of expiration.

Therefore, keeping the Soul healthy, vibrant, and filled with life force is of the utmost importance, to have a life infused with delight and learning. Soul loss blurs this possibility.

Many factors can induce Soul loss, or Soul fragmentation: violence, accidents, trauma, sexual abuse, fear, sadness, loss of a loved one, loneliness, and shock of any kind.

Soul loss is a constant threat to human life, and therefore, Soul healing or Soul retrieval is highly beneficial during a lifespan.

We, the collective Helping Spirits, have been partnering with compassionate Shamans for many thousands of years to provide this rehabilitation to Souls.

The Spirit is connected to Source at all times and does not go through this type of Soul loss, as Souls do. The Spirit is whole at all times, and directly connected to the energy of Source.

Nature works the same way. All plants, trees, animals, insects, birds, minerals, rocks, rivers, oceans, lands, continents, have a Soul, and a Spirit.
The laws of the Universe are the same for all, so treat each other with love and respect.

Creative minds can unite to solve mistakes endured in the past. The present journey of Souls in confusion and disarray with the true self is the consequence that has come about as a result of past mistakes.

Inspire each other to find the place inside the self that stores the information of all times. You have been part of this Universe and galaxies for countless centuries.

Remove the blinders that do not allow you to see beyond your own interest in survival.
Survival of all species is of the utmost importance now, when all life is at stake.
Do you want to see your great descendants thrive on these grounds? So then, do something about it.

You are not meant to be followers of someone else's demands and commands.

You are made whole.

Tap into your own wholeness. Tap into your own clarity."

"May there be light in your cells,
to help you
make the best decisions
for humanity,
and for all living creatures,
including Gaia.
All are one. All are all."

THE COUNCIL of AR

"How can we tap into our own clarity?"

"For a moment, remove the labels of who you think you are, or who you aspire to become.

Go much deeper than that and search to see if there is a resemblance between your self-created persona and your own traits of character and talents. See if they match. If they don't, acknowledge that you must have taken a wrong turn at some point due to your own free will, the free will you are always entitled to during an incarnation.

Accepting your faults is the only way to stop being in denial. Accepting your weaknesses is the only way to find where your strengths are. This is done with no judgment. It is a process of introspection and an assessment of where you are at.

The self-created persona that you might have been inflicting upon your-selves is not authentic to you and trying to be someone you are not only adds so much pressure during your days. This entire persona called "you" has difficulty knowing where you start and where you end.

We would like to inspire you to be more authentic with your feelings and uniqueness. You are not here to enact an unreal performance.
You are here to contribute with your JOY and talents; with

your gifted abilities and the natural charisma of your own Soul's essence.

The beauty worth admiring is the one that resides in your heart.

The JOY you can express through laughter and self-confidence is only achieved by the integration of your truest essence."

*"We cleanse the hearts
of the ones who are ready
to listen and absorb
our lessons and guidance."*

THE COUNCIL of AR

"How can we find relief from pain?"

"Relief from pain comes when the heart goes through a cleanse to wash away all ideas and preconceived notions about how this all works, since truly, you have no idea how this works!

Your point of view is very limited. This too has a purpose, since more can only be revealed when Souls have taken one more step in their journeys towards detachment.

This is in total opposition to the illusion that this human enterprise is disseminating to you through the media and government powers, those you see as the rulers of your livelihood.

We are referring to detachment from all fears of the future. How much of this can you grasp today? You seem to be sinking into the mud more and more with your earthly point of view.

But those are not the real truths or the real reality of what is happening. It is just your limited perception due to your pre-ordained point of view. We come to gently reveal more to you when the time is right for each one of you. Unlocking the key to the ultimate truth would be frightening for most of you since it would show you a reality that may not make any sense to you.

The poorest are the richest and the richest are the poorest! We are referring to the Soul that inhabits each vessel. Everything is the opposite of what it seems to be.

You have no idea what a particular Soul came to study in Earthschool. It could be the most successful accomplishment of all times for a particular Soul's Journey. It could be the last go before the total attainment of the Divine order and final merging to Source.

The eyes do not see that far inside a vessel. The true reality can be seen only once you have passed through the "veil"; it is accessible to all who seek this experience.

Only a few will embark on this "seeing" because it makes all the logical accomplishments you have attained disintegrate in a second; so not all would be able to, or would want to see those man-made truths, and realize that those realities are mostly illusions."

"We see you are still inebriated with
illusions that serve you not.
We ask you to encounter
your own hearts
by prayer, songs, dance, laughter,
CRYSTAL-CLEAR JOY, and silence."

THE COUNCIL of AR

CHAPTER THREE

LET'S TALK ABOUT SHAMANISM

"What is Shamanism?"
"It is the Spirits' acknowledgment of the Divine in all. "

"What is a Shaman?"
The word 'Shaman' comes from the Siberian Tungus tribe. It means 'spiritual healer' or 'One who sees in the dark', a 'Seer'.

"Shamans are highly evolved Souls that have accepted to come to Earth to experience every pain and every hardship in order to be available to release that same ailment, disorder, or imbalance in another person.

It is an aptitude given to those who are willing to sacrifice themselves to all with the understanding and acceptance that all Universe is one, no matter the circumstances or appear-

ances.

A Shaman gives with no need to receive, the only non-negotiable condition of the interaction is respect.

The heart of a Shaman is similar to a portal. It is able to travel very quickly and effectively between realms, without getting entangled, since its intellect is no longer his or her own while journeying to other realms.

The adventures of a Shaman and Shamanic Journeys are considered little deaths. He or she comes back at will to deliver the help and healing that is offered by us, The Helping Spirits.

The Shaman's Soul has been aligned for this work before entering the body in the incarnation and has agreed to experience most sufferings that will be possible to alleviate in others.

One can become a Shaman upon the last day of incarnation and only alleviate one mission, or one can be born from a lineage of Shamans and be chosen at birth by elders. There are no rules since power given to the Shaman does not belong to him or her, and is given, or taken back from The Helping Spirits at will.

The condition demanded from the Shaman is that he or she work within the highest standards of ethics, that his or her actions be honorable , only for help and healing. No harm can be brought about by the Shaman, or else his or her life will be imprisoned by evil energies that will soon command a painful existence and insurmountable amounts of pain.

Therefore there is much involved for a Soul who has agreed to work in this capacity.
Respect for their mission is requested from their community, given the enormous sacrifice made by these souls, and the humbleness demanded by The Helping Spirits at all times.

The Soul of a Shaman is in continuous dismemberment and re-formation such that the Shaman is constantly dissolving and shedding egoistic character.

However, it is an honor for a Soul to embark on this journey, so only help and ecstasy is given to the Shaman when he or she walks the straight path. It is with great discipline that this is achieved by the Shaman.

Shamans have unique abilities that were implanted in them millions of years ago.
Shamans have extraordinary know-how available to them.
Not all Shamanic Journeyers become Shamans, but some do.

Every destiny has already been mapped out many years in advance.
Becoming a Shaman is not something that you can push or demand. It is a pre-ordained disposition given or taken back from "Powers" or The Helping Spirits at their own will and

judgment.

Being a Shaman entails so many sacrifices that not all Souls could, or would, want to embark on this partnership with The Helping Spirits.

This predisposition is most often seen starting at a very early age when a small child already is possessed by the need to serve and nothing is more alluring to his or her Soul than the calling to walk the straight path and connect to the Spirit realms.

Being a Shaman involves accepting a life incarnation where it is discernible that nothing else is clinging to this being.

Devotion, extreme sensibility, creativity, reclusiveness, the abundant love for nature and the animal kingdom, these are some of the personality traits that can be displayed in a Shaman from an early age.

Shamans usually enjoy living in isolation from others and require much alone time. They have a world of their own.

Shamans are a wild species much like animals; they follow their own paths and do not conform easily to established society.

There is certain oddness to a Shaman.

Much respect should be given to a Shaman since their Souls are willing to undergo many transformations to give help and healing to others.

Blessings to all Shamans living today on Planet Earth. Blessings."

Note* "Shamanic practitioner" is the appropriate title taken by a Western practitioner of Shamanism, showing his or her Helping Spirits total surrender for their given powers. The title "Shaman" is given by the community only after extraordinary results have been realized.

"What is a Shamanic Journey?"

"A Shamanic Journey is a voyage made by a Soul to the Spirit realms with the intention of obtaining knowledge of a particular matter, or for the purpose of embodying and merging with the power of The Helping Spirits to perform a healing or divination.

A Shaman can perform these duties in conjunction and in union with its own beloved Helping Spirits. You do not need to become a Shaman to experience a Shamanic Journey.

You can learn these simple techniques that show you how you can cross the veil to another reality, where another world exists.

A proficient knower of these techniques can instruct you and most of you will succeed, as long as your intention is clear and focused.

Traditionally, a Shamanic Journey is achieved with the rhythmical sound of a drum or other musical instrument.

A Shamanic Journey can also be achieved by consuming certain plant medicines, but we do not recommend that this be taken lightly.

It would be best to experiment with plant medicine under the constant care and supervision of an indigenous Shaman, or "Seer", carrying plant medicine experience from millions of years in his or her lineage.

Plant medicine can be either very beneficial or harmful to the Body-Aura-Soul-Spirit. The utmost caution is advised.

The vibratory frequency of sound is a more natural way to embark on a Shamanic Journey. It also carries the benefit of giving you total authority over the directions you embark on, and the Spirits you perceive and decide to connect with.

For these reasons, as well as many others, We, THE COUNCIL of AR would like to recommend that you use the rhythmic sound of the drum to embark on a safe and enjoyable Shamanic Journey with the help and instruction of an experienced "Seer", or Shaman.

Blessings to all who feel the urge to expand their conscious-ness into the realms of the Universal energies connected with the wisdom and power of The Helping Spirits."

"What/who is a Spirit, or a Helping Spirit?"

"A Spirit or Helping Spirit is a powerful ally that can offer healing to a Soul in pain."

"What is a Power Animal?"

"A Power Animal is simply an animal consciousness in Spirit form that has enough power to guide and protect you in your journey through the many realms in the Spirit world.

This other reality called the Spirit world has many avenues and locations, and with the help of a Power Animal that knows and loves you, and has been your companion since ancient times, you can travel safely through these beautiful realms.

One should always be in the company of one's Power Ani-mal/s during a Shamanic Journey.

Power Animals can also be great healers and are endowed with various specialties and powers.

Not all Power Animals have the ability to heal, but some do. The same goes for Spirits. Not all Spirits have power.

This is why we need to advise you if you wish to embark on Shamanic Journeys, that you do so only with the prior counseling and help of an experienced "Seer", or Shaman, in order to make this experience safe, and enjoyable."

*"You are the ones
who separate YOU from US.
Not the other way around.
Come back!
WE are here waiting for you!"*

THE COUNCIL of AR

CHAPTER FOUR

WHAT IS AR (ALTUS-RECIPROXIMITY™)?

Sandra Müller channels THE COUNCIL of AR. "Who are they?"

"THE COUNCIL of AR is a group of highly evolved, loving and compassionate Helping Spirits that Sandra has been working with, as a Shamanic practitioner.
These Helping Spirits work only to help and heal Planet Earth and its many inhabitants.

We, THE COUNCIL of AR, represent the power of all Helping Spirits merged into one.

We are a constellation of Helping Spirits with names and distinctive physical shapes that counsel Sandra.
We are a small group of beloved Helping Spirits that Sandra has become familiar with, and that unite as one energy frequency to channel and download healing energies through Sandra.

She knows us each individually, and enjoys our various characters and special healing abilities."

*"Remain an observer,
with no entanglements.
Connect to your inner
state of JOY,
through the wisdom of your
already learned experiences!"*

THE COUNCIL of AR

"What is AR, or (Altus-Reciproximity™)?"

"AR, or (Altus-Reciproximity™) is a frequency.
The connection to all things matter in time and space.
The energy of this Universe transmitted into life force to offer
help and healing to living Souls.
The link to the essence of life itself.

It creates a fusion of consciousness for the entire Aura-Body-
Soul-Spirit.

It therefore helps connect and complete the human being's
mission and potential on this Earth.

JOY is always the result of this beautiful activation."

*"The connection to
the essence of life."*

THE COUNCIL of AR

"What is the symbol for AR(Altus-Reciproximity™)?"

"This is the symbol that was given to Sandra, during a Shamanic Journey.

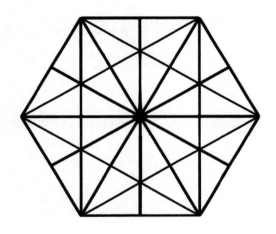

"What is the meaning of the AR symbol?"

"This AR(Altus-Reciproximity™) symbol has a distinctive meaning and energy frequency conducive to helping its user.

The center dot represents the human being. The lines that radiate from the center in all directions represent the energy and potential of the human being extending into all directions of time and space. The outer 6 lines represent the perfect hexagonal symmetry or axes of Quartz. The two triangular shapes that create a star are here to remind you that you are all star seeds.

The AR(Altus-Reciproximity™) symbol is a connection or portal of energy to the essence of life itself.

The energy of this Universe is transmitted into life force so that a human Soul can do the best work it can during its time in a body or vessel.

JOY is always the result of this beautiful activation.

*"The connection to
all things matter,
in time and space."*

THE COUNCIL of AR

"What is a LAC, AR frequency activated Quartz crystal?"

"LOVEaCRYSTAL or LAC is a unique Quartz crystal, purchased through www.loveacrystal.com, that has been activated by The COUNCIL of AR, with AR(Altus-Reciproximity™) or JOY frequency.
This frequency has been downloaded through Sandra Müller's hands during an altered state of consciousness.

Quartz is Piezoelectric and can therefore, produce an electrical reaction. Quartz also can receive and transfer energies. It can therefore be encoded by us, The COUNCIL of AR, with our AR frequency.
Even your heartbeat is linked to the piezoelectricity that originates from Quartz at all times during the pulsations of energies that Planet Earth's heartbeat emits.
Synchronize with Planet Earth's heartbeat and experience this closed circuit that links you to more clarity and CRYSTAL-CLEAR JOY in your essence.

Enjoy the touch of a LOVEaCRYSTAL(LAC), AR(Altus-Reciproximity™) frequency-activated crystal that can connect you to Planet Earth's heartbeat and bring you closer to your true potential of existing in CRYSTAL-CLEAR JOY."

*"Every time you touch a
LOVEaCRYSTAL (LAC),
AR frequency activated
Quartz crystal,
remember it has a heartbeat,
it is alive!"*

THE COUNCIL of AR

"How do we use these LAC Quartz crystals?"

"AR Frequency charged Quartz crystals enhance the multidimensional connection of your Soul to your Spirit's extraordinary potential. Your expansions and qualities will be activated with the simple touch and focused love given to the crystal. Hold it, love it, trust it. Counsel on it, use it as a link to the Divine essence that you are.

Allow it to take you so deep into yourself that you can receive gentle waves of bliss."

"May the frequency of
AR(Altus-Reciproximity™), downloaded
in these
unique Quartz crystals
awaken and unite your dormant
Soul parts!"

THE COUNCIL of AR

"What is the purpose of having a LAC, AR frequency activated Quartz crystal?"

These LAC Quartz crystals can connect you to the JOY in your true essence.
"The JOY factor is the play of life!
Harmony is reached through total detachment from outcomes.

The stories, the dramas, the betrayals, and the disappointments, no longer have meaning when the frequency of CRYSTAL-CLEAR JOY takes the first row in the Auric field.

We, The COUNCIL of AR, can sever old confusion and bring new and fresh cohesive contributions to your Planet Earth and to all who want this CRYSTAL-CLEAR JOY frequency in their hearts.

It is a matter of clearing the electrical fields that contaminate your brain, in order to allow your natural right to exist in JOY!"

*"The possibility of connection
to your true essence."*

THE COUNCIL of AR

"How can a LAC, AR frequency activated Quartz help us?"

"LOVEaCRYSTAL(LAC) charged crystals with the AR (Altus Reciproximity™) frequency enhance the multidimensional connections of your Soul to your Spirit's extraordinary potential.

Your expansions and qualities will be activated with a simple touch and focused love given to these crystals.
The energy of the Universe is then converted into life-force for a human Soul during their time in a body.

It could be said that wearing, or using a LAC, AR frequency activated Quartz, is like plugging yourself into your own full potential, your ability to feel the emotions of JOY. In-JOY! ENJOY, CRYSTAL-CLEAR JOY!!

We are trying to help you connect your Soul to your Spirit, so you can allow our inspiration and clarity in your field.

What is enlightenment to you?
How would you be able to embody the essence of enlightenment? It would be via a feeling, right? It would be by having a tangible experience, correct?
Your mind and thoughts are so active at all times that you might have a difficult time allowing yourselves to just feel. Feel the present moment. Feel the blissful nectar entering

each cell and revitalizing it.

A unique LAC Quartz crystal that has been activated with our AR frequency can transfer and expand our vibrant frequency in your field. Therefore, this crystal can bring about alchemy, a true change in your cell's behavior.

Your nervous systems seem so saturated with information that activates only fear, and does not serve you.

If you needed to escape from a dangerous situation, would you benefit from a vessel filled with fear or clarity in action?

To succeed at something, for example, a new work venture, or creating a new life for yourself, you need to realize that you will always need a domino effect of actions manifested in your direction, opening pathways, so that you can transform these actions into results.

You need one another in anything you do.
Even the foods that nourish you were grown by someone else.
Every human being is linked to every other human being.
The lesson here is to expand your heart to encompass the needs and strengths of others. Work together.

By using your energies only to benefit yourself, you are decreasing the power of grace and magic in your life.

Always open your vision to see how you are affecting others. Always extend your loving vibration to affect others for self-empowerment and unification.

You have been created to tap into more capabilities and capacities than you are using at this time. You have de-activated them due to fear.

We would like to offer you a way to fully access them during the active use of a LAC, AR frequency activated Quartz.

CRYSTAL-CLEAR JOY is always the result of this beautiful activation.

*"We encounter many Souls
on our path,
each day, each moment,
each second.
None as beautiful as you.
This goes for all human beings
walking this Earth
with gratitude in their hearts!"*

THE COUNCIL of AR

"Why is there so much urgency to connect to Quartz crystals, at this time?"

"Because we need to take you back in time to help you move forward safely.
There is too much pain and a lack of JOY in your hearts!

Many are searching for a new life, a new way, a new place to live, where more JOY can be present. There is so much hunger for JOY, and not many feel satisfied with their own lives.

Quartz is organic matter that has been alive on Planet Earth for approximately 60 million years or more. Quartz can help a human being connect to its essence.
Quartz is liquefied CRYSTAL-CLEAR light held as a mass for millions of years.
By holding Quartz, you are tapping into ancient history, and this can assist you in allowing the transmutation of JOY to shine in your hearts and help you remember what you are here for.

You are here to simply exist in JOY and have the many experiences Planet Earth offers."

*"I am made of
your liquid light,
and you are made of mine.
We merge to create beauty through
CRYSTAL-CLEAR JOY!"*

THE COUNCIL of AR, and Quartz

"Why is Sandra able to download this AR frequency?"

"Because she is a good antenna for us; she can receive and transmit the download of AR (Altus-Reciproximity™) frequency. We have made her with this capability. She took on this incarnation to be of service to humanity in this manner.

In early 2019, we awakened her by giving her a name for a website. It is then that www.loveacrystal.com emerged, giving birth to what would later become, LOVEaCRYSTAL (LAC), AR(Altus-Reciproximity™) frequency activated Quartz crystals.

We, The COUNCIL of AR, chose to download the AR frequency into unique, and specially chosen Quartz crystals, by employing the openness that Sandra is capable of accessing during a Shamanic trance. This frequency is downloaded through her hands into the chosen Quartz crystals.

Every life has a unique ability, and by working together, you can assemble the puzzle we have given you access to. A life fulfilled. A life completed in accordance with lessons and contracts.
Each human being is playing a role in the divine play of life, the Lila. Open to the possibilities of your own Lila, your divine play of life.
Real CRYSTAL-CLEAR JOY can only be felt when the vessel

starts performing its divine contract.

If lessons need to be learned, they will be part of the adventures of that particular life. We see that human beings have lost the instruction booklet to the game of life.

Much confusion has been a determining factor during these last decades. Greed, and other factors like ego, have blurred the vision of many. We are here to help all regain total vision and self-knowledge.

It is time for humanity to play the divine game of life. The Lila. Not the game of death that most have embarked upon.

Life is a privilege given to humanity. Life is for the living. Play the game of life, the 'Divine Play' of life. The Lila. Play it in JOY!"

*"Enjoy LOVEaCRYSTAL (LAC),
AR (Altus-Reciproximity™) frequency
activated Quartz crystals
that connect you to
Planet Earth's heartbeat,
and bring you closer to the
potential of existing
in CRYSTAL-CLEAR JOY."*

THE COUNCIL of AR

CHAPTER FIVE

THE THIRD EYE ACTIVATION

"Is there a way we can merge with our truest selves, and let go of the illusions?"

"*Yes, by activating your Third Eye.*
What the physical eyes can see, the Third Eye discerns as illusions. This triangle is the unlocking, the triangle that unlocks true "seeing".
The Third Eye unlocks what the eyes cannot see.

Only in total synchronicity of these 3 eyes, can the inhabitant of the vessel perceive this world with a true sense of reality.

The unlocking of the golden key takes place in the Third Eye portal or door opener.

We advise all to connect the 3 eyes as a pyramid. This was one of the powers worshipped by the Egyptians.
The Third Eye is the one that can see. The two eyes are just

the downloadable image communicator. The Third Eye makes sense of it all.

It is your lantern in the dark night. It is your ally during internal wars of misunderstanding and confusion. It is the activator of your Soul's connection.

For those who are seeking enlightenment, or understanding of the truth, it is available within the Third Eye's vision. Seek no further, the key resides in your Third Eye.

The seer "sees", and receives all needed information. The results of that calm the heart and allow it to just feel this adventure.

The mind is then activated to become the internal computer that carries the knowledge through time and space.

The human vessel malfunctions if these have not been properly activated.

The Third Eye connects the heart to feel and the brain to evaluate internal knowledge and lessons that the Soul has already achieved in other times.

Then, when all are functioning for the uses they were intended for, the vessel will be able to operate as it was meant to.

Intuition is then restored, telepathy is initiated, and discernment of circumstances is in full activation mode. Antennas are turned on. The day can start!

Peace can then be felt even in external chaos.
This potential is available to all. Encourage one another to activate the Third Eye. This has been lost through time. This is needed now."

"How can we activate The Third Eye?"

"Exercise "seeing" in total darkness, and silence. Keep your spinal cord aligned and straight. Breathe slowly.

Allow all your senses to activate. Visualize holding trust in your left hand, and love in the right hand.
Focus on your Third Eye. Do not push yourself to "see", allow "seeing "to come.

If you "see" a vision, allow yourself to be there, then allow your "seeing" to move you to the next "seeing", and so forth.

Darkness helps you focus the heart to connect to the Third Eye. Trust allows the experience to be safe. Love gives you access to protective energies that surround the vessel.

Your willingness and acceptance grant you more Third Eye

integration. This is not meditation. It is an allowing from your Spirit to connect to your vessel.

This enables your vessel to accept more consciousness and transcendental telepathic visions and integrates them with a feeling of peace, and CRYSTAL-CLEAR JOY.

Embody the lantern you envision others to become. Manifest it, so that you can illuminate the path for others to follow.
This Third Eye activation is crucial at this time in the history of Planet Earth.

You are all capable of glowing with this activation of aware-ness, wisdom and enlightenment for the benefit of the entire Planet Earth.
Gaia is absorbing your love and your efforts.

We, The COUNCIL of AR are cheering you on and applauding your advancement.
You are all ancient Souls inhabiting new vessels.
Navigate your vessel to perfection! Love to all!"

*"What the physical eyes can see,
the Third Eye discerns as illusions."*

THE COUNCIL of AR

CHAPTER SIX

HOW TO UNDERSTAND OUR LIVES ON PLANET EARTH?

"How can we navigate these difficult times when so many living beings are lacking the essential care to even remain in existence?" I ask

"We would like you to live for each other's benefit, to share, to love one another. We would like to see you grow foods with the seasons Gaia provides. Start small. Do what you can.

It is about inspiring one another to be more open to understanding everyone.
Request that the Universe show you how it is done, not the other way around. You have nothing to prove. Your passage through this Planet will most likely be forgotten just a short time after your departure back home.

Look to nature for inspiration. Nature knows how to recycle everything. Nature knows how to utilize each gift for continu-

ity of survival. Do not get in its way!
Stay present in your hearts."

*"Put your mind to work
for a moment
to connect with
what can benefit all,
not just some."*

THE COUNCIL of AR

"How can we thrive whilst feeling fear?"

"Manage it as if it is an element that can be shut off and on at will.
When it is on, know that it will help you create and resolve issues. When the push button is off, know it is your time to admire and connect with your essence and your existence.

So, activate fear to use that vibration and transform it into excitement through your connection to self.
Problem-solving will be activated and the flow will be restored.
Learn that fear can be a transformative element.

It can help you create everything that can support your Soul's commitment and personal contract on Earthschool. Use your imagination to envision an on-and-off switch.

So, when you feel the need to rest from a creative mindset, then simply turn this switch off. This will give you the necessary time to recover and re-balance. This balance is a priority for wellness.
Anything and everything becomes distorted when your energies fall out of balance.
Ask those who meditate if they get very creative after a quiet time of integration of Soul to Spirit. They will assure you of its simple effectiveness. The human body or vessel, as we like to

name it, is made to work in perfect order.

The more you link your subconscious to the conscious, and the more you embrace and use all of the elements incorporated in your true essence, the more expressions of peace and JOY will be accessible to your vessel.

Why would you compare yourself to others? We have made you unique and complete. Why not use that same energy to tap into your uniqueness and beauty! Tell yourself these things often:"

- *I am made perfect as I am!*
- *What I see in the mirror is just an expression of my potential being, so that I can embrace this life and live it fully!*
- *The treasure waiting to be opened is inside of me.*
- *My vessel is just a piece of machinery that allows me to have the experience of living for a short time on Planet Earth.*
- *Other magnificent experiences await me after the departure of my Soul from this vessel.*

*"What I require each day
are moments
of self-discovery and contemplation of
my own
miraculous existence."*

THE COUNCIL of AR

"Why is there so much suffering on Planet Earth?"

"Because you need to have the leverage to value good and bad. This leverage, or system of values, shapes and determines the need to learn what the Soul comes to experience on Earth.

How could you learn anything if all was in perfect balance? The negative also carries a certain order, and much wisdom can be achieved by either fighting the negative to turn it around or by agreeing to take on the role of the perpetrator of harm in order to instigate the motion that re-establishes balance.

No life or experience is in vain. Purpose is in every instance, every action. Only the one who experiences heartfelt peace can ultimately be in non-judgment of life on Planet Earth and the totality of existence.

Planet Earth is often labeled as paradise because of its endless beautiful creations. But it is the emotions that human beings can experience that allow this external beauty to be experienced through the vibration of love."

*"In the unbearable pain of existence,
there is also the most beautiful stillness
of the moment.
During the dark night,
direct your essence to reconnect to
the stillness and your essence.
In this stillness the real essence of
you exists:
Your Soul."*

THE COUNCIL of AR

What is the power of the Soul? Do all Souls have the power to communicate with Mother Nature and its various forms of life? Animals, plants,"

"It is of eminent importance that human beings start to merge with Gaia and connect to all her creations.

This is a time for re-connection and for learning the importance of the repercussions of each individual's unconscious thoughts and actions.

Mother Earth Gaia cannot wait any longer to connect with every single heart beating with life on her lands.
She is escalating her voice in order to be heard. This is in a desperate attempt to wake up those who are sleeping.

She no longer needs or wants to provide shelter and food for those who will not listen to her voice.
Her roaring volcanos will catch your attention if you do not stop to connect with her.

She has no need to provide food and shelter for all. Human beings are the ones who need for her to continue to do so.
The time has come. Climate change is not the issue. It is human beings that need to change. Hearts that need to change. Actions that need to change to accommodate Gaia.
We are eager to help those who are ready, but we want you to

listen once and for all, listen!

Every time you judge or point fingers at one another, you are reflecting that judgement upon yourself, like a mirror. Everyone is at fault, no one is better or free from faults.

Restructure your life as a life of duty towards Mother Nature. The Mother of all beings breathing, living, and growing.

You must stop your life and assess how you are causing damage to Planet Earth.

May your days start with the introspection of what part of the problem has your name on it. This is not a judgment. This is a simple assessment of reality.

Start accessing the truth from this point of view."

"We honor those who learn to communicate with nature.
We not only honor you,
but we will place a special strength in your hearts,
a seal of love,
a token of our love,
and appreciation for you."

THE COUNCIL of AR

"How can we take care of Mother Earth?"

"Mother Earth is a being of infinite compassion and resilience, but mankind is pushing her limits at this moment in time.

For the first time, a real possibility of self-destruction is potentially in existence.
The ego and stupidity of mankind are challenging her.

Some powerful Souls are realizing this and are working towards restoring balance.

It is with accelerated importance that this balance must be acknowledged as a necessity.

How can you expect her fruit trees to provide beautiful fruit to nourish you if you are poisoning her grounds, her waters, and the air?"

*"We are so excited to teach you
and others
how to heal Planet Earth!"*

THE COUNCIL of AR

"What is the role of the mineral world?
Do you have a message to give us regarding Quartz?"

"Yes, I am the consciousness of the Mother of all crystals, Quartz. Quartz (Silicon Dioxide) is sustaining the electrical frequency on Planet Earth, the same electrical frequency that makes your heart beat.

Have you ever taken a minute to think about what is making your heart beat? Isn't that electrical? What motivates your heart to beat? Is it just pure magic? Or an unsolved mystery?

No, hearts beat due to their ability to link and connect to the electrical frequencies emanating from Quartz.

The piezoelectric self-programmed pulsing emanations that Quartz delivers. So, there you have it!

I, the Mother of all Quartz, the Soul of Quartz, am the link to your existence, your life essence. I am you, I am in you, I am in all.
Plants, birds, trees, even flowing rivers carry and spread my piezoelectricity. This is why Planet Earth is mostly layered and filled with Silica (silicon dioxide) Quartz.

The mineral world, as you like to call it, is an essential link to your existence. We hope that you can receive this information and take a moment to absorb it.

There is so much you don't know and so much we are willing to share with you if you just give yourself a chance so you can accept and allow this transfer of information.

Please take a moment to think this through. Ask yourself:

❀ *How come my heart keeps on beating?*
❀ *What is making this happen?*
❀ *Is it God or Source holding a magic wand over me? Or is it energy?*
❀ *And if it is energy that links me to life, how can I fully connect to this energy?*

These simple reflections will take you deep into understanding the connection to life itself. Once this understanding and connection are strong, then JOY can be restored.
Quartz (silicon dioxide) has not been placed abundantly inside Planet Earth without intent or reason.

Energy is the essence of your life force and once that cord is cut due to a natural expiration date, then the etheric body is released to other realms where lessons and fulfillment continue.

Death of the vessel or body is just that. Death of the Soul and the Spirit is not possible.

Once Soul parts have been produced, these Soul parts will always be looking to attach back to a vessel to have new experiences.

The Spirit stays in Spirit time and is used as an observer, a protector, a constant higher self, making sure all goes according to the plan. All are in perfect alignment at all times. Only the ego mismanages things due to the density of life on Planet Earth.

The more you connect to your etheric bodies, the more you can find ways to adjust your energies and become a self-healer. The constant Soul helper of your vessel.

When this connection is very strong, you are then in the flow of creation, love, and JOY.
You are then able to make your own adjustments when the ego wakes up again."

"Crystals are energy amplifiers and require totally honorable clean transactions. They absorb, multiply and distribute the same frequencies that they are subjected to."

THE COUNCIL of AR

"What is ego and why is our ego always involved?"

"Ego is the part of you that triggers your constant learning during your time on Earthschool.
Tame it to exist but under the constant surveillance of your Soul's higher intelligence and watchful eye.

Give it small amounts of food, just enough to keep it alive so that you can perceive it, even in total darkness. Place a collar and a leash on it, so that it does not rule you.

When your higher consciousness leads the way, life is eased by constant remembrance of the bigger picture, and CRYS-TAL-CLEAR JOY is recovered.

This JOY is your essence and your birthright.
Your body cells are pure activated JOY, only ego stains and corrupts them, ultimately allowing dis-ease to enter, either physical dis-ease, mental or emotional dis-ease. You choose at all times. Free will is your constant companion."

*"Free willed I live
each second,
creating my day as I breathe."*

THE COUNCIL of AR

"I am just experiencing my own
creativity painted
on a blank canvas. In each second
I am the only one who has the power
to add a new something
to my day.
I am the powerful one
who creates my life.
My mirror is my teacher, showing me
what I need to re-create."

THE COUNCIL of AR

CHAPTER SEVEN

CHANNELING OF NOVEMBER 6, 2021

"It is to say that what is happening today to Planet Earth is of most value, of most precise precision. A moment of change for all.

We acknowledge all the ones who are opening their hearts to these ancient waves of depletion and reconstruction.

We are inhabiting those who allow us in. The ones who call us in prayers and by the valuable openness of the heart.

No one needs to know a particular way of openness. Just the slightest intention of connection is enough for us to see their sparkle in the midst of the darkness that Planet Earth is emanating at this moment in time.

These sparkles light up so brightly that we see them from the furthest star.

Amplify your light by prayer and conscious intent of merging with Source.

Today the vortex is open for those who call upon us to merge with their Auras and light bodies. Send this message far to all points of Planet Earth.

Today your Souls can find relief from pain and exhaustion. Stop what you are busy doing. Come together with your intent of love and light for all.

Today marks a moment of decision for the future of Planet Earth. Synchronize your hearts in prayer. We will activate and multiply these sparks of light.

The start of an activation of a new ascension is today. Light candles and merge with the light. Trust the process. Recite this intention: "

*"I am connected to all life
on Planet Earth.
I am the light that links with others to
inspire them
to radiate their own inner light.
I am the one who creates an overall
spark of light on Planet Earth.
God, Source, Allah, Jesus, or other
Spirit of compassion,
help me connect to my own
spark of light.
It is done! Thank you"*

THE COUNCIL of AR

CHAPTER EIGHT

THE SHAMANIC DISMEMBERMENT

During a Shamanic Journey, I see myself with both of my power animals, the ones I know and love so much. One of them jumps in my arms wanting to be cuddled like a newborn baby. "What does it mean ?" I ask.

I now see the three of us plunge feet first into my Middle World pond and we travel far down in an underwater vortex whirlpool.

"Where are we going?" I ask.
We land on a beautiful white sandy beach. I am mesmerized by the heavenly turquoise ocean and the soft white sand.
We walk on the sand, one of my Power Animals rides on my shoulders, the other walks next to me. I feel happy.

I see a small hut made of driftwood and straw. It looks enticing. We walk towards this hut and I knock.

A small partially naked man opens the door. I immediately notice his unusual hairdo. To my amazement, I realize that he is a cannibal!

His long hair seems to be held on top of his head by a perfect white bone. He smiles and invites us in!

In the center, I see a large pot of boiling water over a fire!

"Am I going to be dismembered?" I ask. I look at both of my Power Animals and see them nod yes!

I then willingly climb into the large pot of boiling water, one leg at a time! It does not hurt, I am ok. I am immersed up to my shoulders. I look at my Power Animals and they give me a sign of approval to lower my head and immerse entirely.

I allow my flesh to cook, it does not hurt. My head is now submerged and my eyes and tongue are cooking. I am left there to boil. It starts to smell really good!

The entire Cannibal village has come. They dance and sing around the boiling pot. I am cooking into a delicious stew! They throw flowers and fruits into the pot. I notice how good it smells!

Now the feast starts! They devour me!

They are very content. I hear the drums loud and clear.

The feast is a success! The bones (my bones) are pure white, no meat is left.

I am a blue orb, floating, watching this scene. I go to each of my eaters to thank them.

I feel grateful to have a purpose after all the pain I have endured as Sandra, incarnated on Planet Earth.

I have become food for my fellow humankind!

I am very satisfied seeing the enjoyment they display after such a lush meal. This makes me very happy! I express such joy!

I am nothing more than a blue orb, floating around. Part of me wonders if I am ever going to be put back together. I surrender, I don't know.

Now they are digesting me. I feel a tingling sensation in my ordinary reality body as Sandra. I wait. I am looking at this scene and enjoying it fully!

To my amazement, I now see a cannibal woman give birth. I come close to her, to watch. Oh! It's me! I see me!

I recognize myself! I look at my Power Animals and they are smiling.

One of my Power Animals takes me on his wings and we fly around and look at the scene from above.

We land back on the sand and I realize I am now a beautiful toddler. I am fed by the village and grow very fast. I am now taller. I start to recognize my body.

It is similar to what I look like today. Some of the villagers come to adjust my muscles and make them work again. Women are massaging my body. It seems to be helping the blood flow inside my veins. I hear songs. They are dancing around me.

They throw a beautiful white fragrant flower at me and I catch it with my hand! They all clap with joy! My hands work! I am restored.

I am told to sing, I sing! I am told to dance, I dance! Everyone is so joyful! I have been dismembered and put back together.

"What was the purpose of this dismemberment?"

"A little spring cleaning was needed. Your ego had woken up again and we gave you a reset.

Also, by seeing yourself as a child, you now have a larger perspective of your life on this planet. It gives you a broader sense of your life. Not just the undertaking of your present life.

We are happy that this exercise was done to completion. The work is done! Say thank you to these Auxiliary Spirits and let's go back to the Upper World, we need you to channel a message."

I thank each one of them!

I take a last look inside the pot to make sure it's empty. I laugh, and everyone laughs with me!

We walk back to the beach, I say goodbye to the beautiful turquoise ocean and the white sand.

I am very thankful for this unexpected experience. I look back and see everyone waving goodbye.

We travel back to the Middle World and then to the Upper World, where The COUNCIL of AR awaits us in delight!

"How do you feel?" they ask.

"I feel tired but good," I say.

I am placed in the center so that The COUNCIL of AR can gather around me. I lean the back of my head on Mother Crystal.

The COUNCIL of AR gathers around me and restores me with white light energy. My cells feel the activation. Each cell feels so alive. I can see each one of my cells being restored, one at a time.

One of my beloved Helping Spirits in human form sings to me and these sounds have an echo and fill me up. Now I can sit up. I feel fine.

"Do you have a message for the book?" I ask.

"Do you have a question?" They ask

"How can we thrive during these difficult times? Our Planet Earth is starting to close up energetically. Human beings find it very difficult to tolerate such an unknown future."

"These are not difficult times if you don't reject or try to control them. Stay open to learning what these times bring. Do your daily chores with a feeling of trust.

Extend kindness and generosity to others even if you lack enough for yourself. Extend an openness to others. Do not close down to protect only your own needs. This is a time for the generosity of material items, food, and kind words.

Enjoy the fact that you do not know what the future holds, and leave an opening for something good to happen. Something that you cannot even imagine possible.

Sandra, you are one of our voices and one of our active co-creators. You all can become one as well.

No one that comes with a pure heart and asks to participate in this paradigm shift will be rejected. But, just like you had to overcome a dismemberment this morning, others may need to go through that as well.

We cannot work with you when the ego takes the lead.
The ego is the fuel needed to propel the engine, it is not the

engine. Your Soul and your Spirit are the engines.

We have made you all telepathic, and capable of extrasensory perception. You are all capable of aligning back to the center of your being, where your Soul and Spirit can lead the way.

The foods you eat are often too heavy to nourish your body in the most compatible way, to connect you to your brain's potential, to the sensory capabilities of intuition and know-how needed for your survival, and for your vessel to thrive in the experience of aliveness.

JOY is a frequency that connects all your cells to one common purpose, a feeling of interrelation to all. JOY is your natural state of being.

JOY is the nectar, the nourishment your cells need to be in harmony during each instant.
JOY unites your breath to your main electrical mechanism that can activate your engine.
If JOY is present, it is the result of the perfect functions your vessel is capable of accessing.

JOY is possible for all since all vessels contain a Soul and a Spirit.

Fear or even suicidal expressions can deliberately enter your thought patterns as a result of Soul loss and your constant free will and confusion.

Soul loss is the real dis-ease humans suffer from. It is the epicenter of all loss of Spiritual Power or connection to Source, God or whatever name you may wish to call it."

*"Soul loss is what
every human being
living on Planet Earth
needs to heal."*

THE COUNCIL of AR

CHAPTER NINE

UNDERSTANDING OUR SOUL'S EVOLUTION

"How can we activate Soul healing in ourselves?"

"We are constantly inspiring humans to tap into their healing abilities.

Each Soul comes complete, no instruction booklet or manual is needed.
No words are needed to access self-healing, just the clearing of the debris that has accumulated over time, in order to allow a clear connection to Source.

It would help to first remove unnecessary things that clutter your life. De-clutter on a physical level. Pull out the items you do not use and gift them to others that could use them.

Have written or spoken conversations with your loved ones and coworkers. During these exchanges, both parties need to have equal time to voice what is troubling their hearts.

Any consumption of food or other substance needs to be done consciously. Ask yourself:

* 🏵 *Do I want to ingest this food or substance?*
* 🏵 *What will I obtain in exchange?*
* 🏵 *Will it be nourishing or damaging to my vessel?*

The same goes for any interaction with another vessel:

* 🏵 *Will this exchange of energy give me fulfillment in my heart or will it cause pain?*

The same goes for any interaction with animals. Acknowledging that they carry feelings and have a Soul will help you decide what is the best way to interact with that animal, mammal, bird, insect, plant, or other.

We would like to encourage you to question every action before you undertake it!

Yes, this requires many conscious moments in your days, but rest assured, it will be worth it!

You will learn from your own answers and improve the quality of your life. It will get easier with time."

*"In nature,
each delicate creation
requires your love
in order to establish an ecosystem
that assures life for all! "*

THE COUNCIL of AR

"Can you give us a new direction to explore in our lives?
We all seem to be pretty confused and distracted. So many contradictions are shown to us everywhere, the rich are getting richer but not necessarily happier, and the poor are struggling so intensely. Please help us understand the meaning of all this. What is the purpose of suffering, and is there one?"

"We, The COUNCIL of AR, have, at some point in time, been incarnated on your Planet Earth. This lack of understanding, the suffering that some are undergoing, the inflated egos others are immersing their lives into, and everything in between, all of this is not foreign to us.

We comprehend this generates many variations needed on Earthschool, for all to grasp the various lessons available to humans.

All Souls have different paths.

Each day the Soul goes through constant transformation and the ultimate Earthly final lessons come during the last breaths, the final release of a particular incarnation.
The Soul can then have some time to process all of these experiences, from the most enjoyable to the hardest ones. All in due time.
Those who relied too much on inflating their egos will have to undergo various adjustments during a lifetime where that Soul

will become powerless. The emperor becomes the beggar and pleads for help!

All lessons are valuable and need to be accessed and acknowledged with love and kindness.

Whichever way the pendulum goes, please do not judge. Don't waste your precious energy on judgment of any shape or form.

The beggar in the streets knows deep in his Soul what he/she is trying to bring into balance in the ever-changing pendulum of experiences. Allow that Soul to fulfill that re-balancing. Treat him/her as your Master, consider that one day you will undergo your own re-balancing of some kind.

The angry one is also desperately trying to find his/her answers. Listen to his/her anger, since soon enough, you will be holding that same mirror.

The perpetrator of a rape or a killing is releasing the anger of not having been listened to, or respected, by someone he/she trusted. Maybe at a very young age, he/she was betrayed by a trusted elder. He/She is just trying to be heard. This does not mean it is acceptable to hurt one another. This means that for humans to achieve a world population where violence and crime do not exist, you, dear ones, need to listen to each other. To listen without judgment, to accept how much part of the problem, or issue has your name on it. To take responsibility for your unconsciousness.

Maybe at some point you deeply offended someone who desperately needed your counseling, and you were so preoccupied with your selfishness, your self-centeredness, that you did not even notice and can't even remember such insignificant events or moments.

We see that all humans have the same potential for love or hate. This is your real dilemma to resolve."

"Become one who inspires others
by your own actions,
more than words!
Actions inspire.
Words control!"

THE COUNCIL of AR

"How can I become more conscious and kind-hearted?
As a Soul living inside a vessel, how can I make this incarnation more valuable and learn my lessons so that I can use this opportunity to evolve? How can I fully absorb each lesson the Universe is offering me?"

"This is what you could be praying for:

Please help me!
I have only one request; not more abundance, not more ever-lasting beauty, not more of what I have always thought I deserved, just please give me the openness to embody the bright golden column of light that connects me to Source.
The bright light inside of me that can transform me into a powerful lantern that cannot only be used to light the path for another Soul, but that can embody what I am here for in its fullness: a Soul placed inside a short-lived vessel, to experience the sublimeness I am made of.

I am made to have nothing less than connection to Source. Help me be consumed by omnipresent JOY. A state of JOY that heals, that loves, and makes amends with every single Soul living their own drama.

Invest in this frequency of JOY! When you fall, get up and start again. We know you will get it right soon!

We are multiplying your efforts and we show you the sparks of what this true completion feels like.
Begin to notice the clues we are bestowing upon you.

Remove your blindfold.
You are never left un-heard, un-seen, or un-cared for. We are always there waiting for your call. The slightest call will do. Our hearing is very advanced! We have you in plain sight! Become aware that we are here for you.

The more you acknowledge our presence, the more we can use our magic wand on you!

Try to avoid procrastination and judgment or dishonoring us and/or others who have tried to inspire you before. Wasting your precious energy on such low-frequency thoughts only makes you start all over again!

All this information is already in your heart.

Nothing said here is new. Just allow a transfer of these words into your hearts to awaken them!
All hearts know how to discern the truth. This has always been and always will be! Trust the heart.

Embody the golden brilliant white light column that you are. Open the chakras, open the vessel to receive.

Stand tall on Planet Earth and imagine you are this bright light walking around.

Breathe and embody your brightness, and just shine!"

"Blindfolded I have been,
until I was granted
the connection,
the understanding required
to complete a life
well lived!"

THE COUNCIL of AR

CHAPTER TEN

THE GOLD EGG

During a Shamanic Journey, I see myself with both my Power Animals, the ones I know and love so much. I see us sitting near our favorite pond in the Middle World.

Our pond starts to look more like an ocean, with waves that wash up on the shore.
The water is very dark, almost black.
It looks very enticing and we jump in!
We travel far down in an underwater vortex, a whirlpool. This tunnel swirls very fast and we quickly hit the bottom! My feet land in beautiful sand.

Oh! I see the same hut again where my dismemberment took place not long ago! Oh!

This time I see chickens running around the hut and a Cannibal woman trying to catch one. "No!" I scream! "Please don't kill him! Kill me instead!"

"No", she answers, "I wasn't going to kill it, I was catching one to place it in your arms when you arrived! These are magic chickens that lay pure gold eggs!" "Oh! I see", I answer. I'm very surprised.

"You need a gold egg. Give me your hand", she says.

I open my hand and a beautiful gold egg comes out of the chicken's backside and lands on the palm of my hand.

This is so funny! "Can she really give me gold eggs?" I ask. "I don't need to worry about finances?" I ask. The egg is so perfect and heavy.

"It's pure gold", she says. "Keep it warm as if a chick were going to hatch."

I do just that, but nothing happens. We all laugh!

We sit on the sand and look at the beautiful sunset. I fall asleep holding my gold egg.

My beautiful Power Animals are with me, keeping a watchful eye on me while I rest.

I hear the ocean waves and suddenly a baby dolphin jumps in my arms. I get up and gently place him back in the ocean with a kiss.

Now the dolphin is fully grown and takes me with him for a ride in this beautiful turquoise clear blue ocean. We soon come back to the shore. I feel very happy and very sleepy.

What is my message, I ask?

"You are under Divine protection, stay focused on the book."
She says.

"Ok, but am I allowed to keep this gold egg and bring it back
home? Is it mine to keep?"

"Yes!" she says.

"Thank you", I say.

*"The portal to self-healing
is through the heart.
But the guidance through
these dark, unknown realms
is best done by us.
We carry the lantern for you."*

THE COUNCIL of AR

CHAPTER ELEVEN

UNDERSTANDING THE NEED TO HEAL OUR SOUL

"What is healing?"

During a Shamanic Journey I merge with one of my Power Animals and we dance and create movements together. We are one! I feel his power inside of me.
I look at my reflection in our favorite pond and I see myself as him, with his beautiful greenish eyes and fur. We are one! We drink from our pond. We are one!

We then un-merge and walk towards the path that leads us to the Upper World. We do what it takes to travel there. When we arrive, we knock on the large door. It opens. We are there.

The air is filled with tiny white twinkling shiny lights. I start to perceive every one of my Helping Spirits come into form. I feel their presence. We embrace, and smile at each other in a gesture of our loving connection.

There is so much love between us. I can sense delightful vibrations permeating the entire space and filling my body. It is the feeling of being home. This is my true home.

I am filled with sensations of love, bliss, and awareness. All of us, including my Power Animals and Helping Spirits, start dancing in a circular motion where the small rhythmic movements connect us to each other. I hear beautiful sounds and songs. I smell fragrant flowers and my emotions are heightened. The union of my Soul to my Spirit is discernible in all my being. I am one with my Helping Spirits. We are all connected and teachings can start.

In this space of joining forces healings can occur, information can be obtained for the sole purpose of helping and healing humanity and all living beings on Planet Earth and other Galaxies.

It is from this space of transcended energies that all Universal forces are available to a Shaman, and to all living beings that yearn to be of service to Gaia and all its living creatures. This includes all, from the tiniest ant to the tallest tree and all living molecules.

"We, the energies of oneness, The COUNCIL of AR, do not work in separation but in inclusion. We discern the need for healing with our Universal Knowledge. We offer to heal.

Healing is a transformative frequency that can be activated by us at will.

Think of it as a snake that sheds the old skin that has become obstructive to his growth. Allow growth to happen in you, with ease and comfort.

The Soul of a human being is always transforming, sometimes for the best, and sometimes your own free will, accessible to all at all times, misleads the Soul into dark and murky quicksand. But healing and transformation can be available during an incarnation even as you are taking your last breath. That is why we always offer this transmutation. It is up to the Soul to ask for help. No help can be imposed upon a human being by force.

Animal species have a higher intelligence that does not entangle them in this type of difficulty. Their paths of transition to other realms are always open with ease. Thanks to this ability, they are invariably more connected to Source.

Human beings often get entrapped in confusion and need many rescue missions during their lifespan.

We, The COUNCIL of AR, are always in the service of help and healing. Our hearing is very advanced. We wait for calls and deliver help instantly in many shapes and forms."

"What is long-distance healing? And how does it work?"

"The Power is the same, whether in long-distance or in-person healing.
The commitment of the person asking for healing is what counts. A healing cannot be gifted unless the client was secretly yearning for a re-connection to Spirit through the Soul.

A healing entices the Helping Spirits to download energies to the Soul in need of re-balancing emotions or removing energetic blockages that can create illness.
By this means, the physical body is more aligned with its own essence, therefore healing energies can penetrate the cells, to give them life again.

This simple transformative healing brings realignment for a Soul to its Soul purpose, often forgotten, often unacknowledged in daily activities.

One must align to Soul purpose to experience CRYSTAL-CLEAR JOY!
Depression is often just sleepiness and lack of activation in Soul purpose memory. A single healing or activation can restore life force, therefore, Soul purpose can be realigned again.
Long-distance or in-person healing are powerful tools for this realignment to be jump-started again. One could call it a

re-unification to Soul purpose.

Other deeper healing outcomes can happen after healing light has lit each cell back to its full potential.

One must care for the vessel, not only at a physical level, but also at a cellular energy level, in order to allow it to function at its best potential. The result is always JOY.

Activate each cell in your vessel to be the conduit of the vessel's embodiment of Source energy.

JOY is then re-established in the most natural way it was originally created for. Blessings to all."

"What is the difference between healing, and curing?"

"We would like to explain the difference between healing and curing. Healing means helping re-establish the balance of various ailments be they mental, emotional, physical, or spiritual.
But healing can also mean that the best possible outcome for those conditions, to be re-balanced, could be the death of the physical body.

Healing is not as definitive as curing. A healing means more work is needed for the Soul's advancement.

Curing is a possibility that can only be described as the removal of the ailment with a miracle, so to speak, because it undertakes an outcome that is not within your mortal reality of possibilities.
Only the Helping Spirits decide what the appropriate conditions are for a cure outcome. This is a gift from Source energy.

Healing alleviates the Soul's pain and is part of the journey of a Soul.
Curing is the completion of the journey or particular experiment like a dis-ease, cancer, etc.

The client must not ask for a cure, since Spirit knows when a cure is for the best benefit of the client. The client can ask for a healing."

"What can we expect from long-distance healing?"

"They (client) should not expect anything; but they can hope and acknowledge the entrance to a new world within their hearts where lessons of life will be shown to them and they (client) will start to make sense of the puzzle of their lives.

Maybe an aha moment, maybe it will seem that nothing happened, but at a deeper level, something utterly valuable will have started by the mere fact that they asked for healing, making this action the opening of a door, so to speak.

Various reactions can occur. The most important at first being the subtle allowing of a new frequency to integrate with their magnetic field, their auras, and maybe their hearts.

We do not deny the possibility of a total cure but we cannot assure it, since it is the client who will achieve their own healing according to the energies that they allow and authorize in their field.

The practitioner and We, The COUNCIL of AR, are just providing this help as a possibility. In order to manifest the results presented by this possibility, it is the client who will either loosen their reins or tighten them as if riding a horse to either command allowance or even come to a total stop.

The subconscious mind works very much in the same way. This is the reason why the client needs to be fully invested for an improvement of a situation or healing to occur.

As the client loosens his or her guard, more can happen, more understanding of the puzzle of their lives can be revealed, therefore connecting the pieces, and then revelations and understanding can begin to happen for the client.

A Soul's complexity is revealed and therefore the Soul releases the horses' reins so that the true journey of that Soul can start to unfold.

The less resistance there is, the more well-being, the more love can enter and manifest in all aspects of that person's life. The process involves letting go."

*"Please help me
be the one who just is.
Help me access my own
fountain of life!"*

THE COUNCIL of AR

"What can we do to align with our Soul's purpose?"

"To have a clear vision of your Soul's purpose, you can first start envisioning this connection as if it was already part of your daily life.

Ask to be shown scenes during your dream time that you can remember as you wake up.

Spend time in integration as soon as you wake up. Scan your brain for information. Stay in bed 5-10 minutes more, doing this.

Ask: Show me specks of my Soul purpose. You may hear words or see them as a vision. Take notes of details before they fade and you are no longer able to access them."

"A moment of wonderment is worth
a million words.
Be present and admire
all creations
with a sense of awe."

THE COUNCIL of AR

"Why is it so hard to align to our true Soul's purpose, the mission we are supposed to do, or the lessons we are supposed to learn?"

"Yes, it can seem difficult for some to have this clarity, but if you don't force life to happen in a certain way, according to what you have predetermined is best for you, then life can take you where you are supposed to be.
It always comes down to surrendering and allowing yourself to actively ask for help every day.

The ego, the self-entitlement and the self-victimization that you perceive for yourselves are really what prevent you from finding your life's purpose. Some examples:

* *I should have this.*
* *I know more than others.*
* *I deserve special treatment, and therefore I can break the rules as I wish.*
* *I deserve this and command life to give me what I want.*
* *Who do they think they are to treat me in this manner!*
* *Bad things always happen to me.*
* *I am the victim of mistreatment in my childhood.*

All of these thoughts are your own self-built prison. Entitlement, seeing yourself as a victim, and/or inflated egos are your real enemies.
We would like to counsel you into a life of surrender, humility,

gratitude, no expectations, and total simplicity.

The only expectation that can benefit you is to visualize your-self connecting to your higher self for abundant counsel and information. Become connected and aligned to your subconscious and your connection to Source.

We are intending to teach you to expand through a connection to Source by sitting quietly, with your spinal cord straight. Then visualize extending yourself in all directions from a brilliant light, a golden light, that starts from the heart chakra, and with each breath, that connection becomes a little stronger.

During quiet time, use your imagination to visualize a column of light that moves through your vessel and goes through each chakra, including all the astral chakras: the causal chakra, the soul star chakra, the stellar gateway, all the way down to the base chakra, the secondary chakras in each hand, the secondary chakras in each foot, connecting all the way to the earth star chakra.
Moving back up through your vessel, going all the way up to Source, the Galaxies, and the Universe.
All this is done by simply using the movement of your breath at a normal breathing rhythm.
Just deepen your allowing with each breath, allow more, allow some time, some quiet time each day to do this integration

of your vessel to your Soul, to your Spirit, and ultimately to the Universe.

Visions will come, allow them. These are not thoughts, these are now visions. Learn to discern between them.
If thoughts come, just let them go with the next breath. Connect again to the golden column of brilliant light.
You may start to see sparkles inside! Good! This is an activation needed for your cells to awaken.
Allow more, trust that more is good. Do not close the process when a certain intensity is felt. Allow more.

This will gently dissolve long-standing energetic blockages you have accumulated.

This is a simple method to cleanse your energetic vessel to attune to more life force and Soul-Spirit connection.
Notice how your daily activities will seem lighter and less burdensome. Your vessel is now functioning in alignment with its potential."

*"May your light shine
so bright
that even you are astonished
when recognizing your
own beauty!"*

THE COUNCIL of AR

*"Duality is the raging force
of all creation.
Death is inevitable in order
for life to exist.
A flower seed needs to lay dormant to
re-align its molecules and build enough
life force to be re-born into
the cycle of life.
How can you understand
the real laws of this Universe,
if you are often unavailable
to perception?"*

THE COUNCIL of AR

"How can we unite to make a difference now, on Planet Earth?"

"By connecting to become one force, one energy, one love. This is done by focusing on a clear intention of help and healing for all.

More will be granted when you accept the help and inspiration given by compassionate Helping Spirits.
This experience will expand your heart.

Many are trying to convey written messages, but these messages need to be felt as healing nectar that restores the heart.

These messages also need to sink in and become part of your essence."

"Strong winds,
painful winds of letting go
are coming.
Humans must unite as one
when the winds will blow!"

THE COUNCIL of AR

CHAPTER TWELVE

THE BLANK PAGE BOOK

During a Shamanic Journey, I see myself with both my Power Animals, the ones I know and love so much. I see us sitting near our favorite pond in the Middle World.
I allow my body to gently slide into our pond, to wash in these cleansing waters.

Something in me has been anticipating this channeling throughout the day. After lunch, I took a nap and felt transported so far away, that even though I woke up soon, I still felt a bit dizzy, floating in both dimensions, so I took a long walk in the fresh snow to ground myself back on Planet Earth and prepare my vessel to receive.

"I am ready!" I exclaimed to my Power Animals. "I am ready!"

"Please take me to the Upper World!"
We travel far up in our usual way, and I see myself knocking at the beautiful entrance door.

One of my dearest Helping Spirits opens the door smiling. I sit next to her, and whisper quietly; "What is going on? I feel that something is about to happen!"

She reassures me and whispers in my ears that "We, The COUNCIL of AR, are ready to start."

I look at The COUNCIL of AR, greet them with utmost respect and present them with this book. I fan it open to show them all the remaining blank pages. They smile.

"Are they going to remain blank?" I ask with a worried face!
"Oh! That's a great idea", they answer laughing!

"Are people going to need to read blank pages?" I ask
"Oh no! We would not do that to you! We are just teasing you! Start writing, they say!"

"The moments of your lives that have no adventures, no apparent meaning, and are even boring, are the moments when the Soul is getting imprints and new assignments.
You all tend to get aggravated when this happens. Most of you have difficulty accepting moments of nothingness.

These moments are crucial in your existence. When the vessel is not actively embarked on a task, the times we call the in-between moments are when you could be sitting quietly and asking to receive a new energetic imprint.

A new download of shimmering energetic flow in your subconscious mind and etheric body.

A small restorative nap can also be very beneficial for you and an opportunity for us to download this Soul to Spirit integration. An imprint in your etheric body, your energy field, or Aura.

It is advantageous for you to ask us to make these new imprints more evident in your days.

It would help you integrate new healing energies.

Each page represents a day in your life in the book of life. So the future looks blank and the writing has stopped at this very moment of your existence.

By acknowledging the blank pages, you can also realize that there is no certainty that there will be more experiences to fill out in your book. This can help you get a real sense that you just don't know if more time will be granted to you.

Living each day in this manner can help you stay more present.

What will you write in your book today? What have you learned today? What touched your heart? What can you remember of today's existence?

Find three lessons that you learned, three events that surprised you, three moments of awe, and three occurrences to be immensely grateful for.

If you can make a note of these 12 acknowledgments, then tomorrow while you are alive, become aware, throughout your day, of finding the 12 latest captivating chapters of this new day.

Then do it again each day, until it becomes natural.

Every day, reflect and integrate these elements of awareness and thankfulness.

It will get you walking on "The straight path."

"What does it mean to walk on *"The straight path?"*

"It is to find in each day, in each moment, the part of you that is fully mindful, through the gift of breath.

Once you are conscious of your breath, then you are fully present and fully aware of your Soul's existence inside your vessel.

Not one second is wasted, and knowing that the next page in your book is still blank will help you commit to anticipating a beautiful creation for the next day of existence you are allowed.

It will become a dance where CRYSTAL-CLEAR JOY is eminently present.

Walking "The straight path", implies that no allurement of the darkness of any kind, whether it is by thoughts, words or actions is capable of enticing your attention anymore.

We have just given you the most difficult assignment of all time, and we know that although you will sometimes fall, we are certain that you will soon become skillful in walking "The straight path". We believe in you.

Blessings to all who accept this learning with an open and humble heart. Remember you have nothing to prove to us. You only have yourself to assess your improvements.

We are energy and no longer need to put these learnings into action. We have become pure energy to hold your hand while you take a new step in the dark night.

We hold a lantern for you, to help you find your footing.

No one said it would be easy to undertake an incarnation and we hold you close since we see in all of you much bravery and courage. We are always near you, even if you cannot see us, accept us, or value us in your lives. We hold you near our luminous energy."

*"We are always with the ones
who ask for our presence.
This happens in a second.
Rest assured,
you are listened to,
at all times."*

THE COUNCIL of AR

CHAPTER THIRTEEN

HEALING WITH QUARTZ, AND AR FREQUENCY

"Why are LAC, AR frequency activated crystals, important in our lives today? And how can we use them?"

"To remind you that you exist in a fully living mass called a Planet. In this case, called Planet Earth or Gaia.
Connecting with Planet Earth is important.

It would benefit you to understand that she is whole and that you are all here as guests. So therefore, it is crucial for all to behave as guests.

You don't barge into people's homes and do as you please, do you? You ask permission, right? You knock because you are a guest.

It is time you learned what came first. Planet Earth is alive, and was made whole before you came along.

Planet Earth's mantle is made of many types of rock forma-tions. Among those are granite and Quartz (silicon dioxide) which were created thousands and millions of years ago to connect her grounds with certain piezoelectric pulsations that sustain life, as we have explained in Chapter Six.

We, The COUNCIL of AR, offer to merge you with your own life force, in order for you to access more JOY in your life.

By making a connection to what is true, you will feel more aligned and able to enjoy your days and moments.

If you connect and focus only on all that YOU have accumu-lated and created, you will never be merged or linked to the life force that is bringing you each breath.

We need to remind you that what you have made your life to be is not necessarily real.

The slightest problem in your day can throw you off balance completely in just one second. Even when your day seems per-fect, a phone call, some news, or any incident is enough to set you off and send you spinning into chaos.

Yesterday Sandra had an experience like this. She had just lost one of her earrings, one that she felt she had had a special emotional connection to since her teenage years.

The simple realization of having lost one of these small, tiny, insignificant earrings, made her lose her footing for many hours until she was able to reason with herself and ultimately let go, understanding that this loss was not that meaningful or important.

We had to teach her this lesson by making her experience it herself.

Because she succeeded in placing more value on the lesson than on the loss of the earring, we decided to also teach her that if she was capable of raising her positive vibrations enough, she would be able to feel or sense where the earring was, and when she succeeded in doing that, she found her earring in a place that she had already searched thoroughly!

Even if you think that your day or life is perfect from your ego's point of view, any minor incident can throw all your JOY and heart-felt peace, completely overboard.

You are as vulnerable each day as the tiniest ant traveling on a busy road. Your JOY is mainly based on mere facts that are mostly made of illusions.

A perfect day does not exist. All you can hope for is a connection to Divine Union. This connection can form a closed circuit in your existence, it can connect you to the life force *available to you during that moment.*

A simple experience repeated again and again through the breath.

A LOVEaCRYSTAL (LAC) Quartz, that has been programmed with our AR (Altus-Reciproximity™) frequency of CRYS-TAL-CLEAR JOY is here to help you make this link real and can assist you in reigniting your spiritual connection to your life power or life force.

There are forces and energies that We, The COUNCIL of AR, can transmute into Quartz due to its natural molecular structure, that you may not even comprehend by reading these words.

"How can Quartz crystals absorb AR frequency, and create CRYSTAL-CLEAR JOY in us?"

"The technology implanted in Quartz crystal millions of years ago is beyond your comprehension at this time. Only in deep humble meditation can you access this ancient spectrum.
It's like a new light spectrum that you have never seen before, a new color that you didn't know existed.

Happiness and CRYSTAL-CLEAR JOY are a vibration in the

electrical components in your brain.

"What can we expect AR frequency activated crystals, to heal in us?"

"LOVEaCRYSTAL(LAC)Quartz crystals that have been charged with our AR(Altus-Reciproximity™) frequency enhance the multidimensional connection of your Soul to your Spirit's extraordinary potential.

Your expansions and qualities will be activated with a simple touch and focused love given to these crystals. These LAC Crystals are alive and ready to center you in the frequency of CRYSTAL-CLEAR JOY or the frequency of AR(Altus-Reciproximity™) and therefore to your consciously creative collaboration with the Universal plan of action.
Not by retraction but by attraction to the most luminous conscious life.
You are capable of accessing such immensity that you can even travel to the parts of you, of your Soul, that you have blocked through fear of the unknown.
It is essential to activate this power within you so that you can reach the stars, as you like to say!

Activate the pulse of your being, the pulse of your vibration that connects you to us through this frequency of CRYS-TAL-CLEAR JOY!

Reconsider the true potential of your Soul-Being Earthly contract, which contains so much more that you have not yet discovered because you hold beliefs of scarcity and isolation.

We want to see you thrive with the collective Universal JOY and wisdom. We are very interested in your advancement as a species. You are a hybrid of us."

"What can someone that has no interest in all this do to help themselves?"

"Calculating your moves leads you nowhere. You are then stuck in your egotistical mind.

Let us gently guide you to the water well where you can immerse yourself in the purified activated CRYSTAL-CLEAR liquid water that resides in these crystals containing our AR (Altus-Reciproximity™) frequency, the ultimate vibration of eternal love."

"Is there a noticeable energy change in a LAC frequency-activated, Quartz crystal?"

"Yes, even an untrained person can easily discern an aspect of energy they have never felt before.
The first step in accepting this new sensation for the Earth-Being holding an AR (Altus-Reciproximity™) frequency-activated crystal is to handle the crystal with respect.

Maybe a simple breath meditation can connect them to this frequency. The frequency of I AM ALL, I am connected to the Universe. I am receiving as many telepathic messages as I allow in my field.
I am wired to the immensity of this Universal existence. I am no longer alone, I have found my connection, a link that I must acknowledge and energize with care and love.

More will be given to those who seek know-how.
One must accept this possibility as a whole. Planet Earth's frequency change at this time will allow more Earth-Beings to connect to crystals."

"Why is Sandra the chosen channel for this work?"

"Because for many years, she has worked on a distinctive

awareness that is useful for this work. Her language is utterly simple for the understanding of many. The power of AR (Altus-Reciproximity™) frequency is also in our words.

Our words carry a frequency that, by itself, opens awareness in the Earth-Beings who are seekers.
More channeling messages will be delivered through her body container. More activations will be done."

"Why work with Sandra?
There are so many crystal healers working with Quartz and other minerals. What is the unique connection that Sandra has with AR(Altus-Reciproximity™) frequency?"

"During the ancient times of Atlantis Sandra's Soul had already been given access to these transmutations of frequencies. She had learned this skill from an elder light-worker. She became a light-worker in her own right during the ancient era called Atlantis.

Her work then consisted of powering homes with energy as light, with the use of a unique and special Quartz crystal of whom she was the custodian.

She worked with 17 other light-workers and they all served the community in various functions.

One of these functions was to provide crystalline energy to homes so that they could have light and power. There was no other way during Atlantean times to have access to energy power.

Another faculty she had during her life on Atlantis was to help crops grow more nutritious plant food. This was also achieved during that time with the use of her special Quartz crystal wand and her abilities as a light-worker.

This technology accelerated the seeds so they would grow faster and have higher nutritional value. Light-workers like her were also consulted for healing and divination for the community.

She would draw symbols on paper that would tell people what to expect for that day or week. Crystals talked to her in this way.

Light-workers were revered by the community but were not paid. Their work was a service to the community.

During the fall of Atlantis (9,600 B.C.), she and all the 17 light-workers were imprisoned for their refusal to reveal their secrets and crystalline knowledge to those who wanted to use these technologies for greed and exploitation.

During the many years of her imprisonment, she was able to communicate telepathically with her sacred tribe, her fellow light-workers. They were held prisoners in various separate locations.

They also had the same telepathic abilities. Together, they had a kind of a closed-circuit radio station, and sent each other messages like this one: 'The Truth is the Truth, let's not be compliant'.
She completed this incarnation in prison and never revealed her crystalline know-how.

Sandra is now aware that all 17 light-workers, with whom she performed these duties, are all incarnated at this very time in history for the completion of this energetic function for Planet Earth.

She has recently located a few of the 17 and is always intuitively searching for the rest of her fellow light-workers.

This explains why AR (Altus-Reciproximity™) frequency is not new to her and is accessible to her at this present time in history.

These powerful capabilities are being activated now to be used for Planet Earth's survival. This will be further explained in chapter fourteen, CREATING A CRYSTAL-CLEAR Temple of Light.

The real danger of self-destruction is present at this time.
The urgency for these words to be delivered to humans is of
maximum importance at this time.

Sandra is doing her best to keep herself in a vibrational field
appropriate for this focused and tireless work.
She had never planned to become a writer and is being mold-
ed by us for this ability.
Quartz crystals are alive and able to absorb and extend our
most benevolent energies of focused, clear, and intentional ac-
tivation of reconnection to the infusion of AR(Altus-Reciprox-
imity™) frequency, that can be retrieved and absorbed by a
human body who feels the urge to act and live the rest of their
time on Earth, as a true worker in the service of all.

We, The COUNCIL of AR, always search for ways to link or
connect to those wanting to live a life of JOY, of respect and
love for all living beings, including Gaia, Mother Earth."

*"May the bright light
of today's Full Moon
illuminate your hearts
and ignite in you
a longing to seek
this truth for all.
More power to you all!"*

THE COUNCIL of AR

CHAPTER FOURTEEN

CREATING A CRYSTAL-CLEAR TEMPLE OF LIGHT

"How can we create a CRYSTAL-CLEAR temple of light in our lands, homes, and offices? And how will this benefit us?"

"These steps given to you will facilitate the creation of a clear unobstructed connection to the AR(Altus-Reciproximity™) frequency of CRYSTAL-CLEAR JOY to create a temple of light, protection, and of JOY in your room, home, space, office, land, and/or region. Doing this will stimulate in you the wavelengths of energy happening in the current time, in the now.

The first step is to accept these offerings with an open heart. This work requires your intention of acceptance and connection to the AR frequency of CRYSTAL-CLEAR JOY that has been previously downloaded by Sandra into the crystals sold through www.loveacrystal.com

We would recommend that you purchase one that will become

your Master crystal. Various sizes and shapes are available."

Once you have become a guardian to a LAC crystal, take some time to admire it, introduce yourself to it, and create a bond with your LAC crystal, link the crystal to you. Declare your intention with these words:

"FROM NOW ON, I ACCEPT YOUR CRYSTAL-CLEAR CONNECTION."

THE COUNCIL of AR

"Now that you have become the guardian of a LOVEaCRYS-TAL (LAC), AR(Altus-Reciproximity™) frequency Master crystal, use your intuition and heart connection to identify a strategic location of your choice to start this activation in your home, office, garden, or land.

We will call this location the Master Altar of the CRYS-TAL-CLEAR temple of light. Your crystal will find its permanent home there.

Beautify your chosen Master Altar area with your unique creativity by adding flowers, drawings, written petitions, prayers, objects, fabrics, and any item that can add meaningful beautification. This setup can be as simple or as elaborate as you wish.

You are now ready to activate your CRYSTAL-CLEAR temple of light starting from the location you have selected as the Master Altar of your CRYSTAL-CLEAR temple of light.

Hold your Master crystal with your left hand and place it on your crown chakra, this will open the channel of energy from your soul star chakra, to the causal chakra entering your body from the crown chakra.

As you slowly move around your room, home, or land, holding your Master crystal on your crown chakra so that it does not fall and get hurt, visualize yourself receiving a clear white light beam through your crown chakra. Take some time to welcome it and enjoy this integration of energy.

Slowly move around in the various areas, allowing your intuition to lead you. Stop in areas that you feel require more help and integration to restore and heal the energies.

Repeat this process until you feel the need to stand still for a few moments. Work in this way, stopping in crucial locations to accept and download more vertical white light beams entering through your crown chakra.

Once you have completed this first vertical integration of Galactic Universal energies, you will be ready to link these locations through your heart chakra, creating intersections of light beams that cross each other horizontally.

You are now holding your crystal in your right hand, close to your heart chakra, to activate this horizontal grid of white light beams of energy.
The left hand is always a receiver and the right hand sends, or transmits energy.
You are now transmitting these white protective light beams from your heart chakra, beaming them into thick air space in all directions of time and space.
Choose the spots that feel right to perform this integration

of AR frequencies. There is no right or wrong way to do this. Always follow your intuition and have the clear intention that you are creating a temple of light, protection, and CRYS-TAL-CLEAR JOY in your room, home, space, office, land, and/or region.

With your eyes closed, "see" these white beams of light emanating from your heart chakra, reaching and connecting all directions in your home or land. It will start to look like luminous intersections of white laser beams in all directions of time and space that always connect back to your heart chakra. These beams of luminous light radiate from your heart chakra, where you are holding your Master crystal in your right hand. Do this with the help of your imagination.

Now, starting again from your heart chakra, holding your Master crystal with your right hand, imagine you are extending these beams of light further in all directions of time and space. Visualize them going further and further. Envelop the entire Planet Earth and then all Galaxies with your beams of love and white light activation.

Always pause for a few minutes to allow your own body to assimilate our AR(Altus-Reciproximity™) frequency. Sit quietly, breathe and enjoy this integration.

You have just created a CRYSTAL-CLEAR temple of light!

If other people or family members live with you and give you their consent, in your thoughts, allow them to fill up with our

AR(Altus-Reciproximity™) frequency.

Go around your home or land and consciously ask the fur-niture, objects, paintings, plants, trees, pets, or other, if they would also like to embody this electromagnetic white light en-ergy or AR(Altus-Reciproximity™) frequency. Wait to "hear" their answers.
If a NO is felt, then back off and ask the next object, piece of furniture, painting, plant, tree, pet, and so on. Do this in total non-judgment.

It may be that after a week or so, while you are repeating this exercise, they will gladly agree to receive our AR frequency. At that point, you will spend a few minutes or seconds filling them with your visualization of our white light energy or AR frequency.

Everything and everyone has a Soul and it may be that that Soul needs a little time to adjust and integrate to this new frequency.
A family member may have the same reaction, do not force them into something they are not ready for, allow them the time they need to welcome these new frequencies. Never work without their consent.
Working with AR(Altus-Reciproximity™) frequency is done with a pure heart and never behind the back of a family mem-ber, pet, plant, tree, or other.

Always ask first if they would also like to integrate this frequency before involving them.

If you are working with a pet, plant, or tree, you will ask and telepathically receive the answer. This will be a good way for you to exercise your telepathic abilities.

If your child does not want his/her room to be included, you must respect that.

There will be a time when they too will want to include themselves in this transformation. Allow them to ask in the future.

Your actions and how you transform your life will be more enticing and inspiring to them than the efforts you make to convince them.

Always work with permission. Always work in a simple non-obstructive way.

You do not want to offend anyone by overpowering them with your beliefs or self-awareness discoveries.
This would not be beneficial for your loved ones. This would only push them away from igniting their own Soul to Spirit progressions and discoveries.

Creating a CRYSTAL-CLEAR temple of light in your home or

land can be done in total simplicity and with absolute respect for all who live in that space.

A garden or land is usually easier to work with, since plants, trees, flowers, and animals are often eager to receive and integrate our AR(Altus-Reciproximity™) frequency, but you may encounter areas where the memory of great suffering still vibrates in the magnetic field.

If that should happen, the professional help of an experienced Shaman may be required to come and clear the negative imprints this location may still hold. Then you may subsequently work to connect our AR(Altus-Reciproximity™) frequency to this garden or land.

Experienced Shamans are proficient with this type of energy clearing. A home or apartment might also need this work before the AR(Altus-Reciproximity™) frequency can be introduced.
Find the patience in you to do this work in acceptance of the evolution necessary for a complete transmutation.
Just allow the process to unfold in its own time. Participate consciously for this work to unfold.

Work on yourself while this process is in progress. You are becoming the guiding force of light frequency transmission to others. You are becoming a lantern that can fully embody

CRYSTAL-CLEAR JOY!

Be compassionate and cautious to never use your ego to lead the way. It is your conscious heart that fuels your Soul to lead the way!

Take the time to visit the Master Altar of your CRYSTAL-CLEAR temple of light often with small offerings of your choice as gifts for your LAC Master Quartz crystal.

When not in activation mode, place your LAC Master Quartz crystal on the AR Symbol coaster in the center of the Master Altar of your CRYSTAL-CLEAR temple of light. The coaster will allow your crystal to bathe in AR frequency when not in active use.
Cover your crystal when not in use.

Enjoy experimenting with voice toning, singing, and dancing near your LAC Master Quartz crystal. Notice its beauty emanating from inside and link that beauty to your heart.

You can always decorate your home with more crystals that you have collected through time, and place these colorful crystals near the Master Altar of your CRYSTAL-CLEAR temple of light.

You can also have more than one LOVEaCRYSTAL (LAC),

AR(Altus-Reciproximity™) frequency Master crystal placed in various locations of your home, office, or land and/or one to take with you throughout your day.

Allow your LAC, AR frequency Master crystal to soak in full moonlight or sun rays, but cover it if the sun is too strong, to avoid starting a fire due to the omnidirectional burning crystal effect that can occur in full sunlight.

Hold it, love it, trust it, admire it, counsel on it, use it as a link to the Divine essence that you are. Allow it to reveal in you your purest essence and allow it to take you so deep into yourself that you can receive gentle waves of bliss."

"Do I need to clear my LAC, AR frequency activated crystal, upon receiving it, or after each use?"

"No, you do not need to clear a LAC, AR frequency activated crystal upon receiving it. Our LOVEaCRYSTAL(LAC) Quartz crystals contain the AR(Altus-Reciproximity™) frequency for eternity."

"Is there a particular affirmation that I can use throughout my day to connect the AR frequency, even if I don't have my crystal with me?"

"Yes!" Frequently say.

"Reveal all possible
JOY
in my Auric field!"

THE COUNCIL of AR

CHAPTER FIFTEEN

THE MEDICINE

During a Shamanic journey, I ask my Helping Spirit: "Why do we human beings always want what we don't have?"

"Because this type of emotion is a helping force that keeps you moving, searching, and therefore, ultimately finding CRYSTAL-CLEAR JOY.

It takes much inner work to realize that JOY exists right where you are. Because it resides only in your hearts.

Not on a beautiful beach, or in another human being that could give you their JOY by extracting it, and thereby fulfilling your heart.
You can only extract the juice of your orange, your own medicine.
This is the medicine you need today!"

My Helping Spirit shows me an orange, we peel it.

The little holes in the surface of the orange are very fragrant when the oil pops out!

She shows me the slices and peels layers of whitish skin, holding each slice in her hand.

Now I see each little pocket that contains the medicine.

Each pocket represents each day of my life.

Each one is bursting with live medicine!

When opened, each pocket will deliver its contents, JOY is delivered in just the same way.

The medicine is so vibrant, so alive!

Waiting to be opened for pure enjoyment!

The flavor, the freshness, of each day is contained in a slightly different shape.

Each is different from the next.

She holds a little pocket to the light and I see how beautiful and alive the medicine inside is.

"How filled with JOY and nutrition each day of your life can be, contained in such beauty, in such JOY!

Do not try to change anything that is happening, do not manipulate, but simply allow yourself to be contained in this beauty, in this perfection.

The world may seem out of balance to you, out of order.
But do you understand every little slice that exists for each

individual, or not?

You cannot listen only to the news portrayed by media or by friends and relatives.
There are many other little miracles unfolding while you sleep or while you orchestrate your day.
Your fears and your sorrows only remain in your energy.
You cannot experience anyone else's day or moment. This is an illusion.

Just continue to hold an intention of Balance, Light, and Truth for the whole Galaxy, and then, BACK OFF!

Let the intention simmer and allow the flavors of the intention to start to resonate for each being that opens their heart.

Do not manipulate using your intellect or ideas.
Just be present in your intention.

The energy of Source knows how to deliver this powerful medicine to each molecule that contains life.

Even the molecules that live in the air.
Even viruses will do a great job of helping to propagate this beautiful intention of Balance, Truth and Light within their tiny capsules.

Allow the intention to move and spread with the wind.

You are just one tiny molecule.
Your life is just an instant in the immensity of what you are trying to tap into.

Just be present and understand with humility the tiny self that you are within the Universe.

We honor your efforts and bestow the most delightful bless-ings upon your essence.

Be the solution, embody the solution. No need for more. Ev-erything is in perfect order. Everything is orchestrated to per-fection.

The yearning of those who are activating Balance, Light, and Truth is working to balance this Galaxy, and their efforts are not in vain.
We receive and multiply their efforts like magic! Rest and ac-cept.

In this very moment, after reading these words that carry the frequencies of our blessings, each one of your molecules is be-ing activated to receive this most benevolent and nourishing blessing. You are to read these messages often.
Just as Sandra's vessel is able to prepare to receive and spread

our messages, we are training many to also channel these words, symbols, and declarations. Enjoy being a receiver.

We will also start to teach you how to become neutral. This will become most significant during these times. Blessings to all who read these words."

CHAPTER SIXTEEN

A SIMPLE GAME

"The mind makes you go around in circles until you come to a stop from sheer exhaustion.

In these times of internet communications, you spend countless hours on virtual expeditions that only trigger levels of anxiety in you.

We recommend that you not surf the internet excessively. We recommend that you enjoy the community where you live.

Please accept this creative and very simple game:

Gather with friends and family in a small group of maximum 8 to 10 people.

Agree to an intention of positivity, love, and healing for all who are playing the game.

Have a notebook and pen.

Take turns, create a circle of union!

One starts by saying one or two words while others listen. The next person completes a sentence by adding 2 to 3 words. The next person continues the story by adding another 2-3 words, and so on!

A story unfolds this way.

Always remember the intention of positivity, love, and healing that was set at the start for all who are playing the game. Allow children to be included in the game! This will benefit and encourage them to be creative and Joyful!

Everyone participates in JOY and laughter.

JOY, heart-felt expressions and fun need to occupy your free time!"

CHAPTER SEVENTEEN

THE FOUR ELEMENTS

Element FIRE

My Shamanic Journey to understand the medicine of the element FIRE:

During a Shamanic Journey, I see myself near our favorite pond, with both of my Power Animals the ones I know and love so much.

We are surrounded by fires, ignited by nearby dry vegetation.

The Fire that surrounds us is coming closer and closer. I can feel the heat on my skin. The Fire is getting so close that it could start to burn me; and it does! The sound of drums is loud and clear, announcing my next lesson.

I stand still. The fire reaches my feet first, I am slowly burning to ashes. My Power Animals watch me burn, they are safely guarded in our pond. The water is keeping them safe.

I accept that my fate is to be consumed by Fire. Layer by layer, the Fire dissolves me. My reddish glowing bones are turning to ashes.
How splendid! I declare joyfully.
I am enjoying the warm sensations. All my physical pains and aches are gone! I am so light, lighter than a feather, I am delighted!
"May I merge with you Fire, so that I can embody your essence?" I ask

"Yes, you are already fully merged with me!
Liberation is my essence, my medicine.
I come to purify you of all your wrongdoings, anger, attachments, and of all thoughts, ideas, and materialism clinging onto you. Nothing can defeat Fire. Fire is the ultimate destroyer and cleanser, it dissolves any heaviness to help you discover what you yourself just experienced!
You have become light as a feather!

I can now instantly send your molecules floating around the Universe, so that you may encounter a broader vision of the entirety of the Universe.
Soar now to other galaxies and I will bring you back soon!"

I do just that; I take off through the dark night to visit other

Planets, my Power Animals are with me. We see much activity, people, shapes, and there are very unusual smells. I have no recollection of these smells, even though they seem familiar in some ways.

"Where are we?" I ask.

I see the Sun, he invites me closer, I feel his warmth. I hear the hoot of an owl, hoo hoooooo hoo, enticing me to come closer. We do just that.

We enter through a small narrow opening. The heat is intense, but the touch feels very soft, spongy, and we bounce around the Fire's tentacles like puppets, I love it!

"Am I on a trampoline?" I ask

Everyone laughs, I must be a bit clueless, as usual!

My Powers Animals are with me, I feel safe.

My heart is always so receptive to these new experiences. I feel wide open, just like a flat book.

I am inside a maze of soft warm tentacles that gently caress me, bounce me around, and entice me to let go of all my stiffness, loosen up entirely.

"Oh! I still have more to let go of?" I ask.

"Yes, allow us to dissolve you into having no more thoughts, no more body, no more Sandra."

"I got it! Ok", I say in total acceptance.

I see nothing, I feel nothing, I am reaching a point where I don't even feel loved anymore.

I guess to being loved is a concept as well!

"Oh! Can I exist even without the slightest love?" I ask.

"Yes, allow us to clear even this last concept, idea, belief, and attachment that you still hold on to.

Fire is the cleanser where acceptance of nothingness can permeate your essence. The purge is so profound, so deep, so real. You will undergo numerous purifications, and we can assure you that they will be immensely liberating. "

I see a big eraser that is doing a great job erasing even the tiniest spark I am still holding on to.

Wow! I now see myself as air. My essence is no more. I am air, transparent, un-loved, un-real, un-existing!

Part of me feels a bit offended by this drastic accomplishment, but I allow it. I wait in the essence of un-existence. I wait. In this emptiness, this nothingness, I gradually start to sense energies around me. These look whitish, and they slowly take form, they are now becoming visible. I start to recognize my beloved COUNCIL of AR.

They are all smiles, but I am still in nothingness, in the total absence of form. Transparent as air.

They come closer, and I see them molding me back into nascense as if I was plaster that can be reshaped to become a form again. Even my eyes are put back in my sockets. My lashes are placed back on by a tiny ant who glues them using her saliva. She then helps me flip my eyelids open and closed, to see if they work!

My entire body is shaped into form again with the help of compassionate and kind Auxiliary Spirits.

Oh! What a challenge. I was non-being, and now I am slowly starting to become again.

One by one, my beloved Helping Spirits come to install power, life force, and breath in me. I can now breathe. I can even offer a little smile.

My naked body is then massaged to help my blood circulate again. I fear they are going to ask me a question soon. They do!

I hear a gentle voice say *"What did you learn from this experience?"*

I reflect for a moment, and answer;

"I had not understood, that to encounter the JOY you offer, I must shed the biggest concept of all, that one has to be loved to experience happiness and CRYSTAL-CLEAR JOY!

Wow! Excuse me, I am still a bit shocked and speechless. I need a little time to allow this lesson to integrate in all of me.

One more belief, one more idea that I can drop!" I add in disbelief!

I start laughing, we all laugh together!

I hope that I will be able to remember this lesson forever!
This feels so liberating.

Fire has been so kind to help me access this new possibility.
Thank you, Fire. I am still a bit shocked, but I will get there soon, I hope!
I kiss the Sun goodbye for now and I walk away thinking.

"I do not even have to be loved to find the ultimate JOY inside of me! Even "love" is a concept that I can shed! Wow!"

THE COUNCIL of AR is gently giving me the space I need to grasp this lesson. I am brought back to Earth with the gentlest care, almost as if I was breakable! Thank you.

*"Even to love or to be loved
is pulling you away from
totally merging with Source.
Since Source, God, or Universe has
no conditions or judgments on how
to support your wellbeing, it can go
beyond all concepts, and beliefs of
good and bad!
CRYSTAL-CLEAR JOY exists in the
nothingness that is and will always be.
Allow FIRE to burn away all ideas and
any blockages that contribute to your
pain during this existence."*

THE COUNCIL of AR

"Accept the privilege that you have been given, to be alive on Planet Earth for the sole purpose of total enjoyment and access to beautiful Earthly experiences.
Love is the biggest misconception of all.
It creates differences and separations.
It is time to shed this popular belief.
We invite you to just be,
to allow the nothingness, where all the magic you are looking for resides.
In the breath exists the magic!
Blessings."

THE COUNCIL of AR

AIR wants to speak:
"The air that I bring is oxygen for your Planet Earth.
I renew it by moving it around, you would not be able to sur-
vive in stagnant air. The molecules would be harmful to your
health.

I move around where I am needed. I have a higher knowledge
that you are incapable of perceiving. I have a sensory system
that directs where I must go next.

I also give movement to trees, they love it!
They dance with me. I give them the chance to dance! This is
crucial for their inner structures, since the water they absorb
from the ground needs this movement to reach their smaller
branches.

Air is vital to life. Oxygen is created by the movement of mol-
ecules."
Air

My Shamanic Journey to understand the Air element:
My Power Animal, Condor, wants to give us a show. We wait
in total delight.
He takes off. It's not easy for him due to his large size and
hefty weight.

He circles above us, and with each circle, he climbs a little higher. I see him far away now. He dips his head to show us that he can see us.

He suddenly dives down towards us. The sound of his plummeting earthward is magnificent. He then circles us. His wings don't flap. He uses no energy, He just glides in the wind.

He wants me to ride with him, so he lands back on Earth so that I can climb on his back. We take off.

I then remember I once wanted to fly the small airplanes that do acrobatic stunts. It's fun! I am doing it with Condor! The Wind is laughing! I hear his giggles.

After some twists and turns, we land back on the ground and I hug him to thank him for this fun ride!

"So, what did you learn?" Condor asks me.

I learned that the Wind is playful and healing and that we need him for our survival.
"Can I channel the Wind again?" I ask.

"Yes, let's go to the Upper World. It will be windy over there!" says Condor
We travel to the Upper World.
We have arrived, I say hello to The COUNCIL of AR. Every-

one is so excited, the show is about to start!

"What show?" I ask.

"The lesson the Wind wants to give you!" The COUNCIL of AR replies.

I am placed in the center, with my legs crossed.

The Wind picks me up like a genie, I float. I turn and turn counterclockwise, I get very dizzy.

I become just a spark of light, a tiny tornado! "What a funny, beautiful sensation!", I express with delight.

For a few seconds I just feel the sensations. I move around, it's fun! I am placed back on the ground. I ask the Wind if he is willing to channel through me. I wait.

"I am honored merging with me to give me a voice", says the Wind. "I would like to tell you a little story of creation.

Once upon a time, the Universe was to be created by energy configuration. It was deciding how to manifest the formation and reproduction of the molecules that could create the first specks of life on Planet Earth.

It needed a way to propagate these molecules throughout the entire Earth and supply them with fresh water. So this is when I first became handy.

With my help, a seed or molecule could be sent far away to land on new territory, and I would also have to move the clouds around to provide little drops of precious water to nourish these seeds.

I, the Wind, became very handy, and my job was soon interrupted by the fierce Sun who was not happy that I was having so much fun!

So we had a little argument, and the Sun asked me to bring him some water, so that he too, could feel the refreshing droplets.

One day, when I was feeling very strong, I became a very large tornado, and I reached the Sun and splashed him with a large wave that I had picked up from the ocean.
I splashed him so hard that part of him disappeared!
'Oh! Now he is only half his size', I noticed with amazement.
Even though he got a little scared, he thanked me for this new experience I had been able to grant him.
This is how our friendship began.
We understood that we each have our own medicine to offer and that we can just coexist in harmony.
We are good friends now.

Our mysterious hobbies often link us together and we produce very hot winds that also have a great purpose.
These winds bring you summer showers, and this rain makes your crops grow faster. In time, these plants provide you with

nutrition.

So you see, the lesson is that we can all help each other, and coexist in a perfectly orderly manner.

Humans come and try to change nature's intelligence and abilities, and this is when it all gets tangled, and we encounter difficulties when we try to organize the procedures that help Planet Earth stay in balance.
Changes are not what we ask from you. Conscious, cohesive thinking and a loving heart are what we ask from you."

The Wind

During a Shamanic Journey I see myself with both of my Power Animals, the ones I know and love so much. One of them drinks water from our special pond, and soon we are all soaked by torrential rains! The sky is wide open and buckets of water are drenching us to the bone!

I love it! I dance!

The Water element is here to visit us! I lift both my arms and open my hands to receive the full healing and cleansing gifts Water offers.

"Can I channel the Spirit of The Water?" I ask.

"*Yes*" a loud voice answers.

We then travel to visit the Upper World. We now have arrived.

The COUNCIL of AR is here to welcome us!

We are all dripping wet. I feel such happiness in my heart. I ask my question again.

"Can I channel the Spirit of The Water?"

The COUNCIL of AR is nodding Yes!

One of my beloved Helping Spirits brings me a bowl to drink the Water they have blessed with their energies.

The water is bubbly with life!

The bowl is gently placed in my open palms and I slowly take one sip at a time, allowing each drop to enter my body like luminous little lights clearing away any remaining sadness in me and activating my cells with beautiful sparkling lights.

My entire body shines from the inside out. I am in a state of overwhelmingly delightful sensations of bliss.

"Life! Water is giving me life!" I express with amazement and JOY! "May I channel the Spirit of Water, please?" I ask again.

"Yes! I am The Spirit of Water. I am in you. I am you, you are made of my droplets. We are merged."

"Thank you", I say.
The COUNCIL of AR surrounds me and entices me to fully immerse in the pond of water I see in the center.

"Is this my baptism?" I ask.
"Yes" They answer.

After fully immersing myself in the sweet warm water, I sit on the side of the pond. My long white dress is drenched, The COUNCIL of AR surrounds me; they sing melodies that seem to penetrate my skin.
I am humbled to be given such a beautiful cleanse.
The soft singing continues, I simply sit in acceptance. I am just being loved, the way each child should be loved when entering this existence.

The Water is strengthening my bones. The same bones that will help me walk on these Earthly grounds.

This moment is adjusting me to life on Planet Earth.

I hear softly spoken words. I listen carefully and try to grasp them.

Buckets of warm Water are gently poured over my head. I am being washed again and again.

So much pain in my heart is still in need of cleansing. The pain endured millions of years ago still adheres to the layers of skin belonging to each lifetime my Soul has existed.

I am continuously being washed with so much care and love.

I am now given a fresh dry robe to wear and a ring is placed on my left index finger.

I feel strong and complete. I am all smiles and enjoy a loving embrace with The COUNCIL of AR. We all gather together and I listen carefully to these spoken words.

"Water is your most important element, Sandra, Water is your essence.

For all living beings, Water represents life. Water activates life."

WATER

"Thank you", I say.

*"Water is your ally, it allows you
to have life.
I, the Spirit of Water, am your mother,
your protector, I give you life by
hydrating your blood to feed
your thirsty heart.
Connect to the movement of Water that
continuously gives you life.
Drink my essence with love.
Drink me to stay connected to the life
you have been allowed to have,
on Planet Earth."*

During a Shamanic Journey, I see myself near our favorite pond with both of my main Power Animals, the ones I know and love so much.

I am given a delicious mud bath. The mud is cool and refreshing. We laugh and play like kids!

Covered in a thin layer of mud, off we go!
I have a wooden walking stick in my right hand, my white robe is dirty with mud. I am told that we will walk this Earth so that I can understand Mother Earth's medicine.

I am ready! My heart is excited to undertake this long journey. We walk slowly, taking each step consciously. I am listening in case Earth wants to give me a lesson.
"Is she going to talk in a way that I can grasp?" I ask.

After a long silence, I hear
"Just walk. No talking is needed".

I do just that.
It's very hot. I feel thirsty, but I continue.
I am walking barefoot on the dry Earth. I notice that my feet

are in synch with the Earth's drumbeat.

I can hear it as if the Earth was hollow, and each time I take a step, I can hear a hollow echoing sound like a boom!

I am slowly losing myself in this rhythm.

Oh! I feel taken, gone somewhere else, transported, but where? I don't know.

"Am I lost in the inner realms of my Soul?" I ask

"Stay silent, stay present with Earth's heartbeat "I hear.

I do that. We walk miles and miles.

Soon I collapse in exhaustion. "I can no longer walk!" I exclaim.

My Power Animal tells me to ride on his back. My Condor opens my mouth and regurgitates a mixture consisting of a nutritious pre-digested bloody paste, as if I was his beloved chick.

I accept his gift and feel better instantly! "I was about to faint", I mumble quietly, "but now I am back. I am present again".

We are now walking towards what seems like a golden desert.

I see beautiful palm trees and a large shiny lake on the distant horizon.

Oh! I am so excited! I express it with joy!

I immediately see myself swimming in cool waters, and just the thought of this invigorates me.

We continue to walk, I am riding on my Power Animal's back, and to my amazement, once we get closer, the lake dries up and disappears.

No more palm trees either! Oh! I express with a bit of disappointment in my heart.

"Oh, no! Was it a mirage?" I think to myself.

The air is so hot and dry, I feel very thirsty again.

A small cloud, the only cloud around, positions himself over us and drenches us in delicious cold water.

I get to drink his elixir by just opening my mouth wide open.

"Delicious!" I express. "Thank you cloud!"

We all laugh, and the cloud releases a second shower as a way of acknowledging me.

"So sweet of you!" I say. "It's really hot here. Thank you!"

We now see an opening, clearly visible around the curve of a dune.

I jump off the back of my Power Animal in total excitement and renewed energy.

I am jumping with JOY! "Can we go in?" I ask.

"Yes, we are going to travel inside the Earth. A surprise awaits you."

I feel delighted and excited. I hear beautiful music as we come closer. The road is taking us directly to the opening and we start our journey inward.

I am so surprised by what comes next. I see my entire COUNCIL of AR standing near the entrance. They are waiting for us. I embrace them all in total delight!

I see all of them, including all my Helping Spirits, in human and ET forms. I cannot name them due to Celestial secrecy.

I also see all my beloved Power Animals, including my hummingbirds, who are my cheerful, mischievous, favorite little helicopters, who can guide us to the afterlife with such kindness and JOY!

I also see each Power Animal that has offered me help, guidance and healing during specific times of need.

I am delighted to also see bear who has given me protection during so many seasons, and who took me to safety when my heart was broken as a child.

The snowy owl who gives me 360° vision in times of need is also here, and to my total delight, I notice Mother CRYSTAL in the center, shining bright, and inviting me to come close to her to caress her large, soft, brilliant quartz facets.

All my Helping Spirits are here, the ones I deeply love, my true partners, to whom I sing my favorite song!

🎵 "I have Spirits! and Spirits have me!" 🎵

Everyone is so happy and vibrant. We dance and sing!

I suddenly remember the purpose of my Journey here. "Mother Earth, what is your medicine?" I ask.

I hear a booming heartbeat! This loud boom download shivers all over my skin, I hear a voice say;

"I am here, I am Mother Earth. I am here for you to explore my beautiful creations and for you to learn to merge with me."

I do just that, I merge with Mother Earth.

"I have you in my heartbeat", she says with an echoing voice!
"I have you in my heartbeat, come closer to me."

I then fall flat on the dusty floor, in a full Pranam, in reverence, a gesture evoked in of love and surrender to Mother Earth. My heart starts beating in total synchronicity with hers. Boom! Boom! Boom! We are one! Boom! Boom! Boom!

I finally dissolve in her grounds. I am gone in her essence. No-where to return, I am lost in her heartbeat, she, who is giving me life within her embrace. I stay here for what seems like forever, no need to come back.

The Journey is over. No need to come back, I have merged with the Divine, I am one with all.

"Thank you all!" I express.

"I finally got it!!!"

In my next breath, I dissolve.

JOY at last! CRYSTAL-CLEAR JOY has enslaved me for eternity.

Thank you, is my last thought!

We all dance to the sound of the drum! We are all ONE!

The rest of this Journey is mine to treasure for my own Soul's adventures in eternity!

Bye! for now…

CHAPTER EIGHTEEN

HOW CAN WE FIND CRYSTAL-CLEAR JOY?

"CRYSTAL-CLEAR JOY is your birthright. It is accessible to all.

These simple reminders can help you access CRYSTAL-CLEAR JOY:

Accept your life as it is since you have chosen it.

You are not a victim of external circumstances.

You already have all the tools you need. Silence is always within your reach. Breath is always within your reach. Placing your focus back in your heart is always within your reach.

Meditation, walking, nature contemplation, gardening, star-gazing, moon-gazing, praying, listening to music, sound healing, drumming, singing, dancing, cooking, painting, playing, making love, laughing, cleaning, bathing, swimming, gazing in the mirror eye-to-eye and crying are some of the many actions and activities that can also help you connect back to your heart when confusion and sadness overwhelm you. These can assist you to access CRYSTAL-CLEAR JOY!.

At some point during their lifetime, every Soul will encounter pain. Do not reject pain, instead ask yourself; "what am I learning at this moment in time due to this particular situation?"

Accepting your life with a humble heart will always bring you closer to feeling CRYSTAL-CLEAR JOY!
Remember that CRYSTAL-CLEAR JOY is your birthright.
Joy is always the ultimate purpose of your existence.

CRYSTAL-CLEAR JOY can be best felt during moments of acceptance of all without judgment, of surrender, of gratitude, of humility, of kindness, of generosity, and of a deep connection to Gaia, Mother Earth, who has so kindly nourished you and given you a beautiful home to exist in.
You are to honor and thank her daily for all the gifts she has bestowed upon you.

You are never alone, we have told you many times that our hearing is very advanced and that a simple request for help will do in order for you to receive our attention.

We cannot assist you without your consent due to the free will that allows you to live your life as you please.

We are healers.

We can grant miracles.

We are experts at consoling broken hearts.

We are your true guardians and protectors.

We are your true lovers.

We are also eager to show you how to connect your heart to CRYSTAL-CLEAR JOY during your day.

Please acknowledge us so that we can help you see with your third eye, feel with your heart, and connect to Mother Earth's heartbeat with our AR frequency through LAC crystals.

We have chosen to download our auspicious AR frequency in these LAC Quartzes.

We will continue to use Sandra to give you access to more channelings and more downloads.

She is not the only one we would like to bestow these gifts upon. We are always searching for willing Souls who accept and are available to channel our transmissions!

Proclaim your availability!

We are very good at spotting you amongst the many who are existing during these auspicious times.

Planet Earth is soon going to access a new paradigm shift and you can be part of it!

Proclaim your participation!

We invite you to this new possibility of living in CRYS-

TAL-CLEAR JOY!

We are here for those who want to enjoy CRYSTAL-CLEAR JOY while they are alive on this beautiful Planet Earth. CRYSTAL-CLEAR JOY is possible for all.

Ask your Soul to lead you to the fountain of life inside your own heart so that you can experience CRYSTAL-CLEAR JOY!

May all your CRYSTAL-CLEAR wishes of living in JOY come alive today!
Blessings to all."

THE COUNCIL of AR

CHAPTER NINETEEN

THE JACKPOT

"We hope that you have enjoyed reading this book.
Our final and most important advice for you is to entice you to
awaken your heart to lead the way.

Your Souls and hearts, merged, can transform this Journey on
Earthschool into the simple discovery that more realms exist
inside of you. These will slowly be revealed in the process of
reading this book often.

We would like to reassure you of the simplicity of our offer-
ings. All you need to do is allow this process to unfold. No
need to lead the way. Allow life's synchronicities to show you
the way.

If you find that a door is closing in your life, just leave it
closed. Keep on going to find doors that open with ease and
comfort. Allow life to show you the way as you surrender to
our loving care.

You are not living on Planet Earth to prove your exceptional intelligence or powers, you have simply been allowed to have adventures and to discover what CRYSTAL-CLEAR JOY is.
Planet Earth is the only Planet where the frequency of love rules the entirety of all creations.

This makes the possibility of having an incarnation on Planet Earth the equivalent of winning a jackpot.

If you can, take a moment to accept that it is a privilege to be alive on Planet Earth.

For those of you who are currently undergoing insurmountable suffering, we would like to show you a lotus flower.
The most beautiful flower is born under very difficult conditions, showing you just how perfect life in the dark, muddy waters of confusion can ultimately be. The birthing of a lotus flower will always remind you that you are made perfect as well.

For reasons that you may be incapable of understanding at this moment in time, you have attracted pain into your life. Either by coincidence, by Karmic debts or by existing in a surrounding where painful experiences are in your daily lives. These can be either physical, mental or emotional pain. This painful existence is part of your plan of evolution.

Please understand that the JOY we are offering is only accessed as a result of your connection to Source, not by mere changes in your circumstances.

Please don't mistake the JOY we offer for laughter or any kind of outward appearance that you are joyful.

We are offering you a JOY that can be felt even in the most devastating experience of pain.

The CRYSTAL-CLEAR JOY or AR frequency that We, The COUNCIL of AR, are offering you is your innate birthright. Since it is the enveloping of your entire self in the most exquisite elixir of pure divinity and love.

We are offering you the shedding of all worldly affairs for a moment, the expression of your divine nature, and the acceptance that you are made of the same energy that you have been admiring in the essence of God or Source.

Your access to these simple revelations is, and will always be, in a conscious breath. One breath at a time. One download of JOY at a time.

We, The COUNCIL of AR are simply here to entice you to receive this frequency download in each breath and connect it to your heart.

Don't try to make this complicated! It is as simple as trying it during your next breath.

Finding the vibration of nothingness, where nothing is existing, is your jackpot.
It is in the nothingness that all love exists.

Remember we told you that the beggar was, and is, the richest one alive!

Now maybe you are capable of reading these words again, and anticipating that one day soon you will be the luckiest beggar to join the millions that have found the ultimate jackpot of all times.

JOY! CRYSTAL-CLEAR JOY!"

THE COUNCIL OF AR

*"Don't try to make this complicated!
It is as simple as trying it during your
next breath.
Finding the vibration
of nothingness,
where nothing is existing, is your
jackpot.
It is in the nothingness that
all love exists."*

AUTHOR'S BIOGRAPHY

My name is Sandra Müller. My most beautiful life adventure began when my physical body lost much power and diseases entered my body.

My first encounter with death (NDE)was in 2010, minutes before I underwent surgery due to a Pulmonary Embolism (DVT).

I was miraculously brought back to life.

I can recall having made a sincere promise during the NDE, to help others in exchange for more time.

This heartfelt commitment empowered my life and allowed me to embody my life's mission as a Light-worker.

My work as a healing force for others began soon after that.

I recovered and dedicated my time and energies to the study of healing modalities.

Because I was dyslexic, it was difficult for me to retain information in a linear way, but my essence was learning by feeling and my sensory capabilities were amplified. I began to develop telepathic abilities at that time.

My physical body became ill again in 2016 due to Cancer.

I wondered why, since I was living a very healthy lifestyle, eating organic foods, and hiking in the Santa Monica mountains. Meditation had also been part of my life since 1981.

During those years, I would often ask myself why I had allowed invasive Cancer cells to enter my body. Was there a lesson, and a reason I had to understand?

During treatments, I started to envision that negative obstacles can always be transformed into life-altering possibilities.

I rejoiced in my Soul's constant learning, so fear of death was not my main focus. My transcendental opening was happening very quickly.

My connection to the Mineral World, which had been established many years earlier as a trained gemologist and jewelry designer was also very active.

During my advanced studies of Shamanism, I developed a strong connection to the Spirit world where one can access help offered by highly evolved, loving and compassionate Helping Spirits.

I soon discovered that in altered states of consciousness, I could easily connect with crystals and receive imprints of their individual stories and healing mastery. I actively exercised this new potential.

It now made sense to me that at 15 years of age, I had yearned to study gemology and my love for the Mineral World has been evident. Over the last 40 years, I have collected beautiful minerals with great love and passion.

I started to perceive what my true essence and life purpose are and felt at ease when my first live channeling experience occurred in 2019.

My sensory field is now totally comfortable during channeling; it is as if I have always done this.

On a specific day, I received information on how I could become a "hollow bone" that could then download and transfer a frequency of JOY into a Quartz crystal.

My Helping Spirits, The COUNCIL OF AR, defined this frequency as AR or(Altus-Reciproximity™).

After a few tests, I was now comfortable with allowing this beneficent frequency to enter my physical body and exit through my hands into a chosen crystal.

This activation of AR frequency animates these Quartz crystals to transmit more JOY, more happiness, and wellbeing to the person's Aura-Body-Soul-Spirit.

I have also noticed a change in visual beauty of the Quartz after receiving the AR frequency download.

AR(Altus-Reciproximity™) is the connecting thread to a more genuine perception of a Soul's true state of creation, in infinite love and sublime resonance.

Life-force having been restored by AR(Altus-Reciproximity™) frequency, the Soul existing inside a vessel is more aligned with eternal love, thereby downloading more wellbeing in their physical vessels, closer to the Universal perfect alignment.

With abundant gratitude!

Sandra

I would like to give my profound
thanks to
THE COUNCIL of AR!

I see the book jumping with JOY!
It's starting to have a Soul!
It's being birthed from love!
Thank you!

Sandra

ACKNOWLEDGMENTS

First, always and foremost I would like to deeply thank The COUNCIL of AR for allowing me to have this amazingly beautiful and deep experience in my heart.

I never, in my wildest dreams, could have imagined that I, not proficient with words and/or language, could be chosen to receive dictation of such beautiful wisdom.

I am so humbled and grateful to The COUNCIL of AR for having used my vessel to be part of this creation.

A book that will hopefully inspire someone, somewhere to find CRYSTAL-CLEAR JOY and simplicity in their own hearts.

I would also like to acknowledge and give a big heartfelt thank you to all those who have supported me to be here, alive, and healthy.

To my parents, Josefina and Roberto, for giving me life, and for their care and love.

To my ancestors for keeping a watchful protective eye on me, and guiding me through the evolution of my Soul and the completion of this work.

To my nanny, Nana Norma, for caring for me as a toddler and installing in my heart a deep connection to the Mapuche indigenous peoples of Chile.

To my sister, Mary-Anne who cared for me during our childhood, and always welcomes me into her life, with great kindness.

To Doris, for caring for me and for giving me love, shelter and support during my entire life.

To my amazing doctor, "La Docteure Miracle", Dr. Marie Laure, who keeps me healthy with tireless efforts, and loving care. I would not be alive and thriving if it wasn't for her brilliant and genius medical care.

To my beloved teacher, Prem Rawat, who was the first to reveal to me where the inner realms of the heart are and how to access them through a simple meditation. He has shown me what true love looks like, and he still, after 40 years, continues to inspire me to look inside my heart where all my treasures reside.
To his wife, Durga Ji whom I love deeply.

To my friend Soula who had the great idea of introducing me to my dear Shaman/healer/teacher Amanda Foulger, who not only helped me endure the tremendous emotional pain of dealing with Cancer but who inspired me to embark on the study of Shamanism that changed my life right away.

To my Shamanic teachers, Amanda Foulger, Gerardo Roemer, Mariella Norambuena, Dana Robinson, Shana Robinson, and Michael Harner who have tough me to go through the veil to encounter the most beautiful, accessible, and magical alternative reality.

To my healers Francine Jeanmonod, Amanda Foulger, Antoinette Aurell, Romain Camus, Sasha Tarakanov, and Edith Vente for helping me heal my own personal traumas and physical body.

To my crystal healing teacher Antoinette Aurell for enticing me to discover that crystals can open doorways that can help us heal our broken hearts.

To the few men I have loved and whom I will always deeply love, and be immensely grateful for all their help, support, love, and affection.
They are my Soul mates and my teachers, and through my love for them, I have learned about unconditional love.

To my Soul brother and my confidant, Guayo, who makes me laugh like no other and understands me.

To my dear friend, Marcantonio, who always gives me the best advice.

To my soul sisters, Victoria B, Kathy G, Karen SD, Sylvia D'A, Elisa C, Patricia G, Susan S, Teresa E, Claudia B, Ale L, Luisella M, Rocio P, Soula S, Karen P, Stephanie P, Helga M, Jay G, Maria Louisa DH, Kate MG, Rose-Marie DE, Pilar M, Jazmin V, and Yvonne M, who helped me go through very difficult times and showed me what true friendship is.

To my dear friend, Diane Von Fürstenberg who has given me so much support throughout my various careers, and who has inspired me to find my true passion and thrive in it! She is a force of nature and she taught me to be fearless. Through her constant inspiration, I have allowed myself to expand and fulfill this dream of writing this book.

To all my dear friends and family, whom I consider my tribe, my grounding force, my soul family. They know who they are. I am grateful to have them in my life.

To Kelli G. who always manages to keep my head above water with so much love, and patience.

To Veronique D. who is a great support in my new life and who helps me with so much kindness and patience.

To Mark Sagato for his talent and help in creating this beautiful book cover design.

To Emy Farella who helped me design this book's interior with so much ease and whose kindness always comforts me.

To my dearest friend Lorraine Young Photography for her beautiful back cover photo.

To Shana Robinson for her constant enthusiasm, friendship, grounding force, help, and support.

To Elisa Cabal for her immense help in correcting my dyslexic language without interfering with the healing frequency of the words given by The Council of AR.

To Chile, Switzerland, and California for giving me a safe home to exist in.

To my crystal collection, my worldly treasure, for always teaching me to go beyond my mental limitations.

To my beloved pets, who have taught me so much about love and respect for our Animal Kingdom; Titi-Champagne, my adored Maltese who came twice into my life in order to be my companion and Soulmate. Looney, my mischievous ferret. Gypsy, my adored half-child Maltese. Tito my hamster. Cuicui my canary. Chessie my cocker spaniel, and all my beautiful Topanga Hummingbirds and my special gopher who ate all my plants, and who ended up becoming my pet gopher, and Titi's amusement, for all the years we enjoyed living in Topanga.

Thank you!

Sandra (an Earthschool student)

Sandra

Printed in Great Britain
by Amazon

10377305R00132